The Black Arcl

WARRIORS' GATE

By Frank Collins

Published May 2019 by Obverse Books

Cover Design © Cody Schell

Text © Frank Collins, 2019

Range Editors: Philip Purser-Hallard, Paul Simpson

For Geoff Carter.

Also Available

CONTENTS

OVERVIEW

Serial Title: *Warriors' Gate*

Writer: Stephen Gallagher

Director: Paul Joyce

Original UK Transmission Dates: 3 January 1981 – 24 January 1981

Running Time: Episode 1: 22m 57s

                       Episode 2: 23m 50s

                       Episode 3: 22m 20s

                       Episode 4: 24m 57s

UK Viewing Figures: Episode 1: 7.1 million

                       Episode 2: 6.7 million

                       Episode 3: 8.3 million

                       Episode 4: 7.8 million

Regular Cast: Tom Baker (Doctor Who), Lalla Ward (Romana), Matthew Waterhouse (Adric), John Leeson (Voice of K-9)

Guest Cast: Clifford Rose (Rorvik), Kenneth Cope (Packard), David Kincaid (Lane), Freddie Earle (Aldo), Harry Waters (Royce), David Weston (Biroc), Vincent Pickering (Sagan), Robert Vowles (Gundan), Jeremy Gittins (Lazlo).

Antagonists: Rorvik, Gundans

Novelisation: *Doctor Who and Warriors' Gate* by John Lydecker. **The Target Doctor Who Library** #71.

Responses:

'The scripts by debut writer Stephen Gallagher expect rather too much of the viewer in terms of being able to work out what is going on from the limited clues provided. The origins of the Tharils, the motivations of Rorvik and his crew, the functions of the gateway, the properties of the mirrors – all are left, to one degree or another, mysterious.'

[David J Howe and Stephen James Walker, *Doctor Who: The Television Companion*, p394]

'With complex concepts and events occurring in different times in a non-linear fashion, it's more abstruse than a Steven Moffat script. Yet, there are clear, strong characters and morals that keep it grounded and accessible. The result is a tour de force of ideas and imagery that, in terms of storytelling and direction, is decades ahead of its time.'

[Paul Smith, *Classic Doctor Who DVD Compendium*, p348]

SYNOPSIS

Episode 1

A spaceship captained by **Rorvik** and carrying enslaved **Tharils** in hibernation is marooned in a zone of 'no space, no time'. A failed attempt to navigate away founders on a time rift which damages the ship's hull and warp drive, and allows the Tharil navigator **Biroc**, himself a slave, to escape into the void outside. Using his affinity for the timelines, he follows the rift to the nearby TARDIS. He opens the craft's doors in flight, accidentally allowing in the time winds, which age both **the Doctor**'s hand and **K-9**. Though out of phase with their reality, he sets all the TARDIS's co-ordinates to zero.

The Doctor, K-9, **Romana** and **Adric** have been attempting (reluctantly in Romana's case) to make their own exit from E-Space, a realm of negative spatial co-ordinates, and return to Gallifrey in N-Space. It seems that the zero interface between E-Space and N-Space is Rorvik's null zone, where the TARDIS now effects a landing. Warning them not to trust the humans from the spaceship, Biroc leaves. While Romana attempts to repair K-9, whose memory hardware has degraded and who now has severe cognitive damage, the Doctor follows Biroc into the white void outside.

The slave ship has detected the TARDIS's arrival, and Rorvik sets out to find it with his second-in-command **Packard** and crewman **Lane**. Meanwhile, the Doctor follows Biroc to a third object in the void: a ruined gothic archway which leads into the great hall of an ancient castle, full of suits of armour, skeletons and the desiccated remains of an interrupted banquet. After Biroc vanishes into a mirror, the curious Doctor accidentally reactivates the suits of armour, which are actually hostile **Gundan** warrior robots who attempt to kill him.

Episode 2

Romana leaves the TARDIS to speak to Rorvik's men. On learning that the TARDIS travels in time, Rorvik assumes that Romana is a time-sensitive like the Tharils, and plans to use her as a replacement navigator. For her part, Romana hopes that the slave ship may contain compatible memory hardware for K-9, so she leaves with them. They connect her to the slave ship's systems, torturing her with electric current to ensure compliance, but she only alerts them to the existence of the archway before losing consciousness. Rorvik takes **Sagan**, **Kilroy**, Packard and Lane to investigate the ruin, first detailing manual workers **Aldo** and **Royce** to start the risky process of awakening the Tharil cargo, in the hope that there will be a survivor they can use as navigator instead. Their first attempt apparently electrocutes a Tharil named **Lazlo**, but he then awakens, unseen.

Adric and the erratic K-9 are separated while attempting to follow Romana, and K-9 finds the Doctor in the banqueting hall beyond the archway. The Doctor has deactivated the Gundan robot, and with K-9's help he accesses its memory. It recalls being created secretly by slaves to be capable of withstanding the time winds, so it could follow and destroy the slavemasters who once owned this place. It reveals that the void domain, the archway and the mirrors are all aspects of the same threshold. The playback is interrupted by Rorvik's party, who arrive to threaten the Doctor. He finds that he is able to pass through the mirrors as Biroc did, but K-9 cannot follow.

Episode 3

Trying to break through the mirrors, Rorvik discovers that they reflect blaster fire, so he orders a large portable cannon, the MZ, to be brought from the ship. Packard and Lane note that the distances between locations in the void are getting shorter. Adric follows them to the ship and finds Romana, who Lazlo has freed. They discover that the ship's hull is made of extremely dense dwarf star alloy. K-9 arrives and gives away their location: Romana is caught by Packard but freed once more by Lazlo, who takes her to the gateway, while Adric and K-9 escape by stowing away beneath the MZ's housing.

Through the mirror the Doctor has found Biroc, who points out that the Time Lord's wounded hand is now healing, and explains that it was his exposure to the time winds that allowed him to penetrate the mirror. The realm beyond the mirror appears to be an earlier period in the building's history, and the feast whose remains the Doctor saw earlier is still in progress. Biroc and the Doctor join it, and the Tharil reveals that in this era his people are the slavemasters, collecting chattels from across the universe, humans among them. Lazlo leads Romana into a mirror, and Lazlo is cured of his burns. They find the Doctor in the banqueting hall just as the Gundan attack occurs, and the two Time Lords are returned to the present-day iteration of the hall, where Rorvik's crew are eating lunch.

Episode 4

Rorvik still wants to access the realm behind the mirrors, hoping that it represents a way out of the void. K-9 arrives and reveals that the space around them is contracting, a process Romana realises is being accelerated by the mass of the dwarf star alloy used to prevent the Tharils from escaping. Speaking privately via a mirror, Biroc warns the Doctor to do nothing. Adric threatens the crewmen with the MZ, and escapes with the Doctor, Romana and the now inert K-9 to the TARDIS. Rorvik tries to use the MZ against the mirrors and finds that its blast, too, is reflected.

Romana is determined to return to the ship and free the Tharil slaves, but the Doctor is more concerned by the realisation that Rorvik is now planning to use a blast from the spaceship's repaired warp engines to break through the mirrors, an action which will be catastrophic in the collapsing universe. They leave Adric in the TARDIS and return to the slaver ship. There, Sagan is attempting to revive the Tharils, with lethal results, but Lazlo kills him and begins to awaken them naturally. The Doctor and Romana try to stop Rorvik from activating the engines, but Biroc arrives and reminds them that they should do nothing. He returns them to the TARDIS while Rorvik exults that he is 'finally getting something done!'

Romana tells the Doctor that she intends to stay with Biroc, to help him in his fight to free his people. The Doctor asks her to take K-9, realising that he will be functional again beyond the mirrors. After they have passed through, Rorvik finally activates the warp engines, and seemingly perishes along with his crew as the reflected blast destroys the spaceship. The catastrophe allows the TARDIS, with the Doctor and Adric aboard, to break through into normal space, while the out-of-phase Tharils leave the spaceship and pass through the gateway. Romana plans to construct a TARDIS with K-9's knowledge and to use it to free the enslaved Tharils across E-Space.

INTRODUCTION

Writers with distinctive authorial signatures, such as David Whitaker, Terry Nation, Malcolm Hulke and Robert Holmes, have emerged from within the established **Doctor Who** series formula that dominated its production between 1963 and 1989[1]. Similarly, a handful of its directors have been identified as 'auteurs'[2]:

> '...whose approach includes a recognisable style, a readiness to adapt the script to [their] own ends, a reputation sufficient that producers and script-editors will angle stories specifically for [them] and a willingness to see working on **Doctor Who** as a challenge rather than a day-job.'[3]

Such figures include Douglas Camfield, David Maloney and Graeme Harper. Arguably, *Warriors' Gate* (1981) is notable despite this, but also precisely because its reputation rests on both Paul Joyce, then an inexperienced, self-described auteur director, and Stephen Gallagher, a writer whose literary signature was still developing.

However, the status of author or auteur within **Doctor Who** is problematic given the multiple modes of authorship usually ascribed

---

[1] Rolinson, Dave, '"**Who** Done It": Discourses of Authorship During the John Nathan-Turner Era' in Butler, David, ed, *Time And Relative Dissertations In Space*, pp176-177.

[2] French critics writing in *Cahiers du Cinéma* in the 1950s developed the auteur theory, wherein a director was the sole author of a film based simply on artistic ability and vision rather than on writing, casting or production.

[3] Miles, Lawrence, and Tat Wood, 'Which are the "Auteur" Directors?' in *About Time: The Unauthorised Guide to Doctor Who #5 – 1980-1984: Season 18 to 21*, pp59-63.

to the production of the series, where many others in front of and behind the cameras are recognised for their own contributions to a particular story. *Warriors' Gate* is, then, an example of how authorship in **Doctor Who** can be seen as neither entirely the privilege of its writer Stephen Gallagher nor its director Paul Joyce, but also as the collective responsibility and agency of a production team and the result of several factors impacting on the overall narrative of season 18.

While *Warriors' Gate* demonstrates that 'collaboration was ingrained in the process of "authoring" **Doctor Who**'[4], authorship was and continues to be credited to individual writers, producers and directors elsewhere in cinema and television. In television there are many whose names generate specific authorial expectations. For example, we often refer to a 'Dennis Potter play', designating him with a specific signature as an author who addressed recognisable personal themes throughout the body of his work. Similarly, in describing an 'Alan Clarke film', we acknowledge a reputable director making television and films with a recognisable social agenda that embody his shooting and editing styles. In the same terms, **Doctor Who** producers are both venerated and damned by fans as the signifiers of particular periods in the production of the series. *Warriors' Gate*, for example, is part of the 'JN-T era', a decade spanning 1980 to 1989 when the producer was John Nathan-Turner, whose role was tied closely to the programme's growing and vocal fan base, and who, as a consequence, became the target of criticism for its perceived failures, including falling ratings, in the mid-to-late 1980s.

---

[4] Rolinson, '"**Who** done it"', p177.

Stephen Gallagher is credited as author of the scripts that constitute *Warriors' Gate*, but it's well documented that script editor Christopher Bidmead and Nathan-Turner helped Gallagher shape the first drafts of those scripts via meetings, telephone conversations and letters. In steering the series, both also brought their own agendas into play. Bidmead ensured scripts arrived by the agreed deadlines and fulfilled his briefings to the writer. He was responsible for making those scripts work within the context of television drama narrative and production at that time. Nathan-Turner probably had less influence on how scripts were rewritten in his first year as producer, even though he had commissioned David Fisher's *The Leisure Hive* (1980) and had edited his scripts prior to Bidmead's appointment, but he determined and shaped the changes to the series through his choice of directors and writers, casting suggestions, budgetary and resources management, publicity and his presence during post-production editing and dubbing. One of the aspirations of his first year as producer was to bring in directors who had not worked on **Doctor Who** previously and could bring fresh ideas to the series as it entered the 1980s.

As Gallagher completed his third drafts, director Paul Joyce joined the production and, although he recalls there only being a 12-page treatment[5], archive paperwork, retrospective articles and interviews suggest he acknowledged receipt of not only the original 25-page treatment but also the second draft scripts, and provided Gallagher with notes about the latter. Given Gallagher's lack of experience of writing for television, Bidmead and Joyce rewrote and restructured the scripts for rehearsal room purposes and television studio

---

[5] **Toby Hadoke's Who's Round** #165, 'Paul Joyce Part 1'.

production. Bidmead asserted that *Warriors' Gate* 'needed to be taken to bits and rewritten from top to bottom to make it dramatic. That's what Paul and I did. I did all of the typing and contributed 50% of the ideas.'[6] This remains open to interpretation when Gallagher's ideas, descriptions, characters and certain scenes and dialogue remain intact in the final rehearsal and camera scripts. However, in comparison with the first draft scripts, the rehearsal scripts do reveal the substantial work undertaken by Bidmead and Joyce to rewrite and reorder scenes and dialogue, streamline the story, strengthen cliffhangers and clarify the central concepts.

Gallagher, Bidmead and Joyce all agreed that the scripts needed to be edited and structured to make them dramatically coherent. Gallagher was disappointed when he saw their:

> '...final cut-down of the material to a bare-bones version that would translate into a shooting script. In places, they did things that I would never have done [...] I took it as a personal judgement on what I had written.'[7]

Further to this, executive producer Barry Letts also provided notes on Bidmead and Joyce's scripts, generating further rewrites, and they continued to make changes as the story went from rehearsal to studio. It can therefore be appreciated that authorship could be assigned to more than one person, given the structure and nature of

---

[6] Griffiths, Peter, 'Fifth Man In', interview with Christopher H Bidmead, *Doctor Who Magazine* (DWM) #258.

[7] Cook, Benjamin, 'In Space No-one Can Hear You Scream', interview with Stephen Gallagher, DWM #295.

BBC production at the time where the provenance of authorship was continually shifting.

It becomes just as complicated to assign authorship of *Warriors' Gate* to director Paul Joyce, given that he not only rewrote the scripts in partnership with Bidmead and Gallagher, but also had a freelance artist and an entire crew providing ideas on everything from sets to costumes, music and visual effects. While Joyce certainly provided notes on Gallagher's second draft and was paid for rewrites, Gallagher deemed it highly contentious for him to take credit for certain ideas in those scripts.

Indisputably, Joyce's individual approach to the mise-en-scène, the shooting and editing of *Warriors' Gate*, is a thoroughly tangible visual representation of Nathan-Turner's 'search for modernity in season 18'[8] and the story stands out as a unique expression of what **Doctor Who** could represent when an auteur filmmaker attempted to bring a cinematic sensibility to a standard multi-camera BBC studio production, made on a small budget and under considerable time pressures. Joyce's direction of *Warriors' Gate* is situated within the more complex definition of auteur theory developed by critics Andrew Sarris, Geoffrey Nowell-Smith and Peter Wollen. For them, the work of an auteur is distinguished by the technical competency and personality of the director and the discernible interior meaning of a film. Furthermore, authorship should include the director's conscious and subconscious use of Hollywood genres and narrative structures[9].

---

[8] Rolinson, '"**Who** done it"', p186.
[9] Wollen, Peter, *Signs and Meaning in the Cinema*, pp143-50.

There is a school of thought alleging that Joyce was unable to continue at all because of ill health, and that this left both production assistant Graeme Harper and Nathan-Turner responsible for directing some scenes during one of the studio recording blocks. Other members of the production team also considered Joyce either an unsuitable choice as director or overambitious and too inexperienced to cope.

However, despite these prejudices and several production problems, Joyce demonstrated it was possible to innovate within the restrictions of a studio-based drama. While industrial disputes were beyond his control, it could be argued that other internal conflicts he encountered, as a result of trying to apply his sensibilities to the studio recordings, arose because he lacked the clout of more established and experienced directors who had cut their teeth on studio-based and filmed drama. Many television directors like Philip Saville, Alan Clarke and John McGrath embraced experimental, non-naturalistic styles in their early work and, unlike Joyce, had the benefit of long careers working with sympathetic producers within the BBC. They had learned to fight for and exploit the studio system to their advantage and push beyond its conventions. If the BBC hierarchy and structure of the time was the proverbial round hole, the inexperienced Joyce was certainly the square peg trying to fit into it and, similarly, it could be argued that the shifting relationship between director and producer, which allegedly resulted in Joyce being fired and re-hired several times by Nathan-Turner during the recording, inadvertently affected his career progression as a director in television.

The opening chapters of this study focus initially on the significant influences and experiences outside of **Doctor Who** that Bidmead,

Joyce and Gallagher brought to bear on their authorship of *Warriors' Gate*. Gallagher's concept emerged out of a British science fiction tradition undergoing many changes; one that had, by the late 1970s, embraced a textual hybridity, incorporating other social and cultural ideas that broke down the genre's conventions, and as a result become more experimental and abstract. To shape the trajectory of season 18's overall narrative, Bidmead took a similarly abstract approach to current scientific thinking. He embraced many of the themes and concerns addressed by this new wave of science fiction, particularly its fascination with the idea of entropy created by the slow disintegration of the social, economic, ecological, technological, cultural and political legacies of the 1960s. The first three chapters conclude with a look at the various drafts of the scripts and the contributions made to them by Gallagher, Bidmead and Joyce, as part of the discourse on authorship that continues to surround *Warriors' Gate*. Finally, the remaining chapters explore the wealth of Joyce's avant-garde and modernist theatre, film and cultural experiences and influences and how, during production, these nourished and illuminated his interpretation of the existential sensibilities and the cinematic references in Gallagher's scripts.

CHAPTER 1: 'A MEDIEVAL MYSTERY PLAY'

Although John Nathan-Turner had many years of experience as **Doctor Who**'s Production Unit Manager, his boss Graeme MacDonald, the BBC's Head of Series and Serials, was cautious about appointing him as its relatively inexperienced producer during the internal merger of the separate Series and Serials departments in 1980. To that end, he invited Barry Letts, **Doctor Who**'s former producer, to support Nathan-Turner as an advisory executive producer during season 18's production. Ironically, Nathan-Turner said he'd had 'huge ambitions to be Barry Letts'[10] when he later recalled his experience working as a floor assistant on *Colony in Space* (1971).

To replace former script editor Douglas Adams, he and Letts interviewed freelance journalist and writer Christopher H Bidmead after receiving an endorsement from prolific writer-producer Robert Banks Stewart. A former actor and graduate of RADA, Bidmead began writing radio plays while performing as a member of the BBC Repertory Drama Company. He had also written for television, including episodes of Thames' daytime dramas **Harriet's Back in Town** (1972-73) and **Rooms** (1974-77) on which Banks Stewart had worked as a story editor and associate producer. Bidmead was writing scripts for industrial films and contributing pieces to *New Scientist* when he wrote to Banks Stewart, praising his much-loved private eye series **Shoestring** (1979-80) and seeking out writing

---

[10] Nathan-Turner, John, 'The John Nathan-Turner Memoirs Part One: It's Not Where You Start…', DWM #233.

opportunities. It prompted Banks Stewart's recommendation of Bidmead to Nathan-Turner.

Reluctant to take the job, Bidmead recalled of **Doctor Who** at the time: 'I went away and watched some, then came back and said I didn't think I was right for it, because the whole thing was frankly really rather silly.' Coincidentally, this reflected Nathan-Turner and Letts' concerns about the previous season produced by Graham Williams and script-edited by Adams. By returning it to its educational remit and using science to inform the stories, Nathan-Turner and Letts wanted to distance the new season from the self-aware satirical tone set by Adams who, Bidmead suggested, 'had spent the 70s making **Doctor Who** sillier, in his own brilliant way.'[11]

One consequence of Letts' view that the series had been relying on magic rather than science to tell its stories was that Bidmead was given a remit to 'put the scientific method at the heart of the show, giving the Doctor a spirit of rational enquiry and getting him to solve problems through observation and hypothesis rather than by using his sonic screwdriver or K-9.'[12] This remit included the departures of Romana and K-9 as Nathan-Turner felt it was time to change the 'seemingly-invulnerable line-up of the TARDIS crew.'[13] However, the pervading sense that Bidmead applied 'pure science' to the stories under his purview misreads his more conceptual approach. When Bidmead introduced the E-Space theme linking three stories in the season, he wanted to rationalise what he saw as the arbitrariness

---

[11] Arnopp, Jason, 'Science Friction', interview with Bidmead, DWM #407.

[12] Toon, John, *The Black Archive #15: Full Circle*, p22.

[13] *Doctor Who: The Complete History*, Volume 33, p52.

that had crept into the format, to drive the storytelling by synthesising scientific concepts and morality tales based on conflicts faced by the Doctor. He regarded **Doctor Who** as a distinct form of drama:

> 'The central thing for me was that the show [...] was a medieval mystery play. [...] I did see the thing as a battle between good and evil with the devil appearing on the left-hand side of the stage and God appearing on the right-hand side of the stage and the conflict happening between them. [...] I think probably philosophy rather than pure science was what saw me through that season...'[14]

Bidmead wanted to explore the morality play concept within the philosophical aspects of science, 'embracing not just numbers and theorems but a whole glut of other influences including social sciences like psychology and sociology, literature, music and even architecture.'[15] He may have been influenced by several popular philosophy of science and mathematics books of the era, probably familiar to him through his work on *New Scientist* and his long-standing interest in science and technology.

These included Fritjof Capra's *The Tao of Physics* (1975), which examined theories of the subatomic physical world within 'the consistent and beautiful philosophical framework' of Eastern mysticism that concerned itself with non-action, change and the harmony of the universe [16]. Douglas Hofstadter's book on

[14] **Toby Hadoke's Who's Round** #148, 'Christopher Bidmead Part 2'.
[15] MacDonald, Philip, 'Change and Decay', DWM #185.
[16] Capra, Fritjof, *The Tao of Physics: An Exploration of the Parallels Between Modern Physics and Eastern Mysticism*, pp12-13.

mathematics and creativity *Gödel, Escher, Bach: An Eternal Golden Braid* (1979) was the inspiration for some concepts in Bidmead's own scripts. Its ideas ranged from mathematics creating meaning from the meaningless (as in *Logopolis* (1981), for example, where block transfer computations create solid objects out of nothing or delay the effects of entropy on the universe), to the concept of recursion (seen in the Escher-inspired, mathematically constructed environment that looped in on itself in *Castrovalva* (1982)[17], or the ghostly Watcher that prompted the Doctor to create his future self in *Logopolis*).

More relevant still was *Wholeness and the Implicate Order* (1980) by theoretical physicist David Bohm. During the redrafting of *Warriors' Gate*, Bidmead sent Gallagher a photocopy of an interview with Bohm[18]. In the *Sunday Times* interview, Danah Zohar suggested that Bohm, Professor of Theoretical Physics at Birkbeck College, had ruffled a few feathers with his theory of the implicate order. His book proposed 'a world view that gives a coherent understanding of physical phenomena, and it suggests that both the material world and consciousness are parts of a single, unbroken totality of movement.' The article provided an illustration of a man watching two screens on which a fish, filmed in a studio, is seen from two

---

[17] A central inspiration for Hofstadter's book, Maurits Cornelis Escher (1898-1972)'s notion of recursion, as visually represented in Bidmead's story, is also best seen in his later works 'Relativity' (1953) and 'Ascending and Descending' (1960).
[18] University of Hull Archives, UDGA *Warriors' Gate* (file 1). Letter from Bidmead, 29 July 1980, enclosing a copy of the *Sunday Times* interview.

different points of view. The implicate order theorised that 'reality is not merely the two separate pictures he sees on the two screens; it tells him that both pictures stem from a single source – the events in the studio.'[19] When Danish artist Louwrien Wijers interviewed Bohm in 1989, he explained:

> 'Everyone has many experiences of this implicate order. The most obvious one is ordinary consciousness, in which consciousness enfolds everything that you know or see. It doesn't merely enfold the universe, but you act according to the content as well. Therefore you are internally related to the whole in the sense that you act according to the consciousness of the whole.'[20]

This theory embraced a holistic, often imperceptible, view of the universe, where everything and everybody is connected together. This was akin to Eastern spiritual philosophies that embraced a 'wholeness', and in direct contradiction to what Bohm saw as the fragmentation happening in Western society and scientific thinking.

Bidmead aligned this with his concept of E-Space, the Charged Vacuum Emboitments (CVEs) that allowed access to it, and other ideas that Gallagher introduced into *Warriors' Gate*. These included the collective consciousness of the Aboriginal Dreamtime, the *I*

---

[19] Zohar, Danah, 'How the Universe Hangs Together', *The Sunday Times*, 27 July 1980.
[20] Wijers, Louwrien, 'Art, Dialogue, and the Implicate Order' in Nichol, Lee, ed, *David Bohm On Creativity*, p130.

Ching[21], and a race of time-sensitives that could pre-visualise a universal consciousness. Bidmead later acknowledged:

> 'I myself was tinkering around with the *I Ching* at the time. I'm very interested in the concept of a holistic universe. Everything that goes on in the universe, including the random fall of a coin or [...] bamboo sticks [...], tells you something about the universe.'[22]

Although Bidmead believed that magic was the inverse of science, his concepts, where even mathematics could be similar to a magical incantation, seemed to embrace the metaphysical and the philosophical interpretations of science popularised by those authors.

Bidmead was also aware of the writers reshaping the science fiction genre in the British New Wave[23]. One of their overriding concerns was entropy – both as a scientific theory, as seen in the second law

---

[21] The *I Ching*, also known as the *Book of Changes*, is an ancient Chinese divination manual that uses cleromancy (the random use of coins or yarrow sticks) to generate hexagrams, based on six numbers, the permutations of which can then be looked up in the manual. These provide guidance to decision making. The roots of Tao and Confucian philosophy are said to have their foundation in the *I Ching*.

[22] Bidmead, Christopher, 'The Dreaming' documentary, *Warriors' Gate* DVD release.

[23] The British New Wave (named in homage to French cinema's 'Nouvelle Vague') was inaugurated during Michael Moorcock's reign at *New Worlds* magazine from the mid 1960s to the early 1970s. It linked science fiction to current scientific theory, philosophy, psychology, pop culture and the avant-garde.

of thermodynamics, which states entropy increases with time, and as a philosophical 'state of the nation' discourse about the increasing corruption, chaos and decline within society in the 1970s. This cultural pessimism generated a pervading melancholy in the British New Wave, as identified in the work of Christopher Priest, M John Harrison and Keith Roberts, connected to the sense of 'an end-time, with the post-war settlement unravelling.'[24] Again, this equated to the melancholic atmosphere of season 18 and the idea that the fourth Doctor's tenure was slowly decaying and about to fold in on itself. *Warriors' Gate* – as hard science fiction **and** a fairy-tale – is 'an explosion of all the themes explored so far in the season, its most vivid images revolving around the decay and rejuvenation of history.'[25] The human and Tharil empires fall and rise in cyclical, yin and yang patterns and associations: in the crude, worn out warp technology of slave traders shown in contrast with a quasi-mystical form of time travel used by former slaves to restore their empire; in a tired and cynical crew of humans – who depend on rational action – faced with an outer void where events and actions are apparently shaped by random chance; and where the quantum theory of universes folding in on themselves is intertwined with the poetic, metaphoric imagery of French cinema.

A dearth of workable scripts meant that Bidmead urgently needed new writers with new ideas before he could introduce his remit to the series. He approached several, and also decided to resurrect 'Sealed Orders', a story commissioned in 1979 from Christopher

---

[24] Luckhurst, Roger, *Science Fiction*, pp175-80.
[25] MacDonald, 'Change and Decay'.

Priest[26] but eventually abandoned by Douglas Adams on his and Williams' departure from the series. Bidmead admired Priest's work, as it mirrored his desire to tell science fiction stories with a conceptual, philosophical bent. He requested a scene breakdown of 'Sealed Orders' on 27 February 1980 and, considering it as a possible conclusion to the E-Space trilogy of stories, briefed Priest to include the departures of Romana and K-9. As Bidmead started working with Priest, he met Stephen Gallagher, a writer who had been brought to his attention by radio producer-director Martin Jenkins. Like Priest, Gallagher had not written for television before and their similar lack of experience would prove to be problematic.

Gallagher, inspired by his experiences during his last year reading Drama and English at Hull University, first opted to find work in the film business in London to gain experience in film editing and directing:

> 'I'd been one of the student directors on the TV audio-visual course and I'd written a half hour play [...] it was two tramps after the apocalypse. So, it was kind of thieving from [Samuel Beckett's play] *Waiting for Godot*, thieving from science fiction, thieving from anything I could lay my hands on basically. That, I'd really enjoyed doing...'

Gallagher eventually met producer John Fairley, who introduced him to BAFTA award-winning current affairs documentary producer John

---

[26] Priest's first novel, *Indoctrinaire* (1970), a Kafkaesque exploration of time slippage, initiated an award-winning writing career. *The Inverted World* (1974) describes Earth as a city planet that moves along on rails in a time-distorted pocket universe and weaves in themes of entropy.

Willis at Yorkshire Television. Gallagher became one of his researchers but, after a few weeks, he took the offer of a job at Granada Television as an assistant transmission controller. His full-time responsibility at Granada was for the continuity and scheduled play-out of programmes in the transmission control room. However, in his spare time he developed his career as a writer and became involved in collaborative projects with voiceover actors and in-vision continuity announcers. This ad-hoc repertory company included announcer Chris Kay who, like many in the group, went back and forth between Granada and Piccadilly Radio, Manchester's first commercial Independent Local Radio (ILR) station, looking for voiceover and advertisement work. He eventually facilitated an introduction to Piccadilly's commercials producer Tony Hawkins[27].

As well as a remit for local news and current affairs, entertainment and arts, sport, religious and children's programmes, the acquisition and renewal of the ILR franchises overseen by the Independent Broadcasting Authority (IBA) required the provision of radio drama. Gallagher became the de facto writer in a consortium comprising local actors, announcers, producer Hawkins and the station's breakfast DJ, Pete Baker. This consortium pitched a six-part science fiction radio drama, **The Last Rose of Summer**, to Piccadilly Radio in 1977.

Gallagher developed **The Last Rose of Summer** from a short story, 'Stand Up and Be Counted', written in 1974 and submitted to a readers' competition in *Science Fiction Monthly* (one he did not win). An early version of **The Last Rose of Summer** expanded on the dystopian Britain described in the short story. A computerised

---

[27] **Toby Hadoke's Who's Round** #166, 'Stephen Gallagher Part 1'.

command centre has learned to reproduce and program itself and has enslaved and brainwashed London's population, who have become indolent through the lack of productive work and an excess of mundane leisure activities. The concept of one man defying this machine logic and infiltrating and shutting down the programs of one of the vast machines enslaving society, by dint of his awakening intuition and imagination, went on to form the central narrative of the radio version. In it, the innocent but dissatisfied Mitchell uncovers a set of manuals that reveal how the machines were able to demarcate human society into an elite of idle citizens and an underclass that scrapes a living in the city's crumbling underbelly. Alerted to the knowledge that has come into Mitchell's possession, police inspector Randall is ordered by Central Command to eliminate him. After a pursuit, Mitchell infiltrates Central Command and, injured in a failed act of sabotage, confronts Randall with the truth before he dies. He leaves Randall to shut down the program.

Transmitted in 1978 [28] , **The Last Rose of Summer** was very successful. Both Gallagher and Piccadilly Radio were praised in the IBA's Annual Report[29] and it reached the last four in the single plays

---

[28] Broadcast dates for these ILR radio serials remain elusive. A 16 December 1977 internal Piccadilly Radio memo about the £500 budget for **The Last Rose of Summer** from producer Tony Hawkins, filed in the Hull Archives, places recording of the serial as early 1978.
[29] *Independent Broadcasting Authority Annual Report and Accounts 1977-78*, p35. The chapter on local radio reported 'some encouraging progress […] on the broadening of ILR entertainment programming' with the commissioning of 'local playwright Steve Gallagher for six half-hour plays on a futuristic theme under the title of **The Last Rose of Summer**.'

and serials category in 1978's Imperial Tobacco Company and Society of Authors awards. The serial also fulfilled Piccadilly's promise to produce drama:

> '…here was, on its doorstep, a very, very cheap piece of drama that they could broadcast. So, they then went and sold that drama to all the other companies on the Independent Radio network that had made the same kind of promise on their franchise applications.'[30]

The Last Rose of Summer wasn't intended as the first part of a trilogy, but Piccadilly asked Gallagher for more. It also generated a novelisation for Corgi, the paperback imprint of Transworld Publishers. Of this break into radio and publishing, Gallagher reflected, 'It was really the act of writing the radio scripts that took me across the line from wannabe into writer, forced me to go the distance, forced me to discover how to make it all work.'[31] Two further Piccadilly Radio serials, produced by Hawkins and Baker, **Hunters' Moon** (1979) and **The Babylon Run** (1980) greatly expanded Gallagher's universe.

Hunters' Moon has ex-police officer Randall, banished to a labour camp in the Arctic, encounter an imperfect 'robot' simulacrum of Mitchell, created by an alien race that intends to invade and asset-strip the Earth using a loyal army of programmed humanoid simulacra. The aliens reveal that Randall is their ultimate simulacrum, a perfect duplicate, programmed to replace the real Randall. He and Mitchell switch off the alien programming, the

---

[30] **Toby Hadoke's Who's Round** #166.
[31] Gallagher, Stephen, email to author, 28 April 2018.

invasion is foiled and they and the simulacra, no longer loyal to the aliens, head off into space to find a world to settle on.

In **The Babylon Run** Captain Ella Desmond and her crew bring their ship, damaged after a warp jump through a black hole, to an abandoned, empty asteroid hotel orbiting the dying sun Persephone. The hotel, about to be destroyed by a meteor strike, is actually a hidden military installation, situated in a buffer zone between two competing power blocks, and is preparing to defend itself against any incursions. Discovering it only functions militarily when inhabited by human life forms, Desmond and her crew abandon the hotel in an attempt to shut it down. Failure to do so will leave it activated, and cause political turmoil and an intergalactic war. Willis, one of the low-grade Spacer technicians who maintain Desmond's ship, is a non-human simulacrum. He recognises the approaching meteor strike as Randall's ship, 'full of heartsick machines, all coming home to die'[32], and that it will drag the hotel with it into the sun. Willis stays behind as the humans depart, tired of his immortal existence and intent on suicide, knowing the hotel and the ship will be destroyed.

The ILR radio trilogy marries the corruptive effects of power and control, including the enslavement and abuse of artificial beings, to an exploration of human and machine identities and sentience. Mitchell, Randall and Willis inhabit a post-human, biotechnological world where humans and machines, in a Faustian pact with power politics and militarism to extend life and consciousness, become interchangeable and indistinguishable. In depicting a future where technology penetrates so deeply into individual identities it causes

---

[32] **The Babylon Run**, episode 3.

an existential crisis and schizophrenic condition, Gallagher anticipated the cyberpunk movement's concerns with 'not only the interpenetration of human and machine but also the potential decoupling of self from body.'[33] The concerns about control, and the fluidity of the slave and master relationship between humans and machines, transfer to Gallagher's history of the human and Tharil empires in *Warriors' Gate*, of the former slaves becoming the masters and, centuries later, vice versa. The Tharils are themselves hunted down by robots and subjugated by biotechnology, forced to link with machines in order to visualise a navigable route for the slavers' privateer.

Between 1978 and 1980, while still working at Granada, Gallagher wrote for Piccadilly Radio, published the first radio serial as a novel, completed two film tie-in novelisations, wrote his novel *Chimera*[34] and submitted spec script *The Humane Solution*[35] to the BBC's Radio Drama department. John Tydeman, a key figure in BBC radio drama, directed the latter, and encouraged Gallagher to submit a serial format and storyline called 'The Wingmen' for **Saturday Night**

---

[33] Luckhurst, *Science Fiction*, p213.

[34] Predating *Warriors' Gate* (written January-August 1980), *Chimera* went through a long gestation between 1979 and 1980 before publication by Sphere Books in 1982. On the back of its success, Gallagher revised his novelisation of **The Last Rose of Summer** and optioned novelisations of **Hunters' Moon** and **The Babylon Run** (both abandoned by Corgi) under the pseudonym of Stephen Couper. Sphere published *The Last Rose of Summer*, retitled *Dying of Paradise*, in 1982 and *Hunters' Moon* as *The Ice Belt* in 1983.

[35] Broadcast 17 March 1979 in **Saturday Night Theatre** (1943-98), BBC Radio 4.

Theatre. He found it 'utterly fascinating' and 'an original, gripping story, which made me long for the conclusion!' and he passed it on to others in the department for their consideration[36].

Retitled *An Alternative to Suicide* (1979), its director Martin Jenkins, like Tydeman, was another fervent supporter of Gallagher's work: 'he obviously enjoyed the fact that my stuff was anything but social realism, and that it gave him opportunities to push the medium in all kinds of unusual ways.'[37] *An Alternative to Suicide* develops and extends, very effectively, the themes of the ILR serials and, in particular, focuses on the exploitation of the dehumanised, conditioned Spacers, the underclass of grease monkeys introduced in **The Babylon Run**.

Lesterman, a Spacer conditioned by drugs and hypnosis, is on a deep-space exploration mission aboard the *Iron Star*. An accident triggers deeply buried emotional responses that force him to question the motives of the Company that indentured him as a child. After some shore leave, he rejoins the *Iron Star* and warns an officer, Lydecker, against mistreating the Spacers. Seeing him as a threat, Captain Delisle sends Lesterman on a dangerous first contact mission.

Lesterman and another explorer, Pickford, are abandoned near a nearby black hole with no apparent means of returning to the *Iron Star*, and argue heatedly about bringing the Company to task. Lesterman decries a humanity 'obsessed with the trash of the moment [...] Squeezing a dim shadow of happiness out of material

---

[36] Hull Archives, UDGA *An Alternative to Suicide* file. Letter from Tydeman, 23 September 1978.
[37] Gallagher, Stephen, 'Creating the Audio Drama'.

goods that rust and rot and fall apart, and really believing that these things have some actual importance.' He predicts that 'The market economy that produced the *Iron Star* isn't remotely interested in gaining a new perspective on man – it's only looking for something new and bigger to exploit.' Pickford encourages the self-pitying Lesterman to return and challenge the Company, arguing that 'living, however difficult you may find it, is the only counter to that slow death' that is 'Entropy [...] the slow disintegration of the universe.'[38]

Lesterman links with an alien machine that maintains a gateway through the black hole. On their return to the *Iron Star*, Delisle confirms that the mission is a sham because the Company has already deemed a first contact situation as financially unviable. Instructed to kill himself, Lesterman instead triggers the Spacers to revolt against Delisle. Lydecker is reinstated to command the mission and meet the aliens who created the gateway.

'My early work was fairly derivative SF,' was how Gallagher summed up this period when he wrote seeking representation by an American agent[39]. It's a rather modest assessment of his work within the context of the significant changes British and American science fiction underwent in the 1960s and 1970s. Gallagher's lengthy correspondence with writer Andy Lane provides an insight into the influence of particular writers on his radio work and the development of *Warriors' Gate*:

---

[38] *An Alternative to Suicide*, broadcast 16 November 1979, within **Hi-Fi Theatre** (1978-79), and repeated 19 November on BBC Radio 4.
[39] Hull Archives, UDGA *General Correspondence* (file 3). Letter to Kirby McCauley Ltd., 19 July 1984.

'I had the standard infatuations with HG Wells and Edgar Rice Burroughs; I can't really read Burroughs comfortably anymore, but Wells' stuff seems to have held up for me. [...] Harry Harrison's *Bill, the Galactic Hero* is one of my favourite books – along with Joe Haldeman's *The Forever War* it brought home to me that contemporary issues could be covered in SF without detracting from its scope.'[40]

While the satirical tone of *Bill, the Galactic Hero* permeates the ILR serials, Haldeman's *The Forever War* (1974) is more influential, given that it explores imperialism, the nature of military hierarchies, and the impact of technology on identity and consciousness.

The cycle of war and a never-ending military service perpetuated by near-immortality clearly influenced aspects of *An Alternative to Suicide* and the historical loop of human and Tharil conflict, and the rise and fall of their empires, described in *Warriors' Gate*.

Gallagher also acknowledged the influence of Alfred Bester's *The Demolished Man* (1953) on *Warriors' Gate*[41]. A hybrid of science fiction and detective novel, Bester's story features telepathic police officers, Espers, who can predict and stop crimes before they are committed in a society where premeditated murder is a thing of the past.

Like Bester and Haldeman, Gallagher explores the search for human identity beneath the cloning, cybernetic augmentation and

---

[40] Hull Archives, UDGA *Warriors' Gate* (file 1). Letter to Andy Lane, 19 February 1981.

[41] Cook, 'In Space No-one Can Hear You Scream'. Gallagher praises Bester for offering 'such amazing glimpses of the future.'

psychological conditioning of his main characters. He makes them symbolic of how ordinary citizens are manipulated by corrupt authoritarian governments and greedy corporations. Paul Joyce also picked up on the theme of entropy in Gallagher's work, visualising the dilapidated privateer of *Warriors' Gate* as undertaking a job that has been 'put out to tender, and the lowest tender has got the job and we're in it.'[42] The story also depicts the corrupt and cynical human enslavement, through technological means, of a time-travelling alien race that was, in the darkest chapter of its history, just as cruel to humanity. Gallagher's concern with the enslavement and exploitation of individuals, communities and societies as a symptom of technological progress, is also connected with real-world advances in computers, genetics and biotechnology.

These narratives sit within the context of SF as 'a literature of technologically saturated societies'[43] and a corollary to the historical impact of technology on human life, culture and subjectivity. Programmable computers and early iterations of the internet also raised concerns in the genre about the gradual erosion of boundaries between human and machine. By contrast, Bidmead was inspired by the arrival of the home computer in the 1980s. Not only was he one of the few writers creating and editing his scripts on a computer, but several related themes emerged in *Logopolis* and *Castrovalva* when 'he became fascinated by the relationship between society and computers and by the concept that we might all be fictional ourselves.'[44]

---

[42] Joyce, Paul, interview with author, 3 August 2018.
[43] Luckhurst, *Science Fiction*, p3.
[44] MacDonald, 'Change and Decay'.

As Gallagher's immortal simulacra and conditioned Spacers underwent existential crises in his radio dramas, similarly, the British New Wave was exploring a future of human beings augmenting their bodies and consciousness by technological means, and an introspective view of society, using entropy and chaos as a metaphor for 'social or personal disintegration and dislocation.'[45]

Gallagher's work, particularly its focus on the relationship between the human and the machine, also evokes the concerns of two German philosophers, Martin Heidegger and Theodore Adorno. Heidegger's existentialist reading of technology's impact on human beings posited that by dominating the world and nature through technology and automation, humanity would reduce itself and society to a commodity. Adorno also saw mass culture as another form of capitalist machine enslavement where work and leisure became interchangeable and human imagination was simply grist to the technological mill[46]. Imagination and initiative are almost eradicated by Central Command in **The Last Rose of Summer**, drowned out by leisure activities demanding blinkered conformity. **Hunters' Moon** reveals Earth is simply a commodity to be exploited by aliens using an army of programmed simulacra. Human slaves in *Warriors' Gate* develop robot technology to hunt down their Tharil masters. The Tharils become surplus to requirements once they've served their purpose as navigators, and the privateer's cynical crew, operating a ship that barely works, care little for their Tharil cargo beyond its market value.

---

[45] Baker, Brian, *Science Fiction: A Reader's Guide to Essential Criticism*, p77.
[46] Luckhurst, *Science Fiction*, pp87-90.

Finally, it's worth mentioning Gallagher's use of the word **simulacrum** in this context. French sociologist Jean Baudrillard theorised that we lived in a 'hyperreality' where it was no longer possible to tell the difference between physical reality and simulated reality, human and artificial intelligences. He defined a 'simulacrum' as a version of reality that gains its own truth, citing Disneyland as an example of what Umberto Eco referred to as 'the absolute fake.'[47] There are echoes of this in the future society of Bester's *The Demolished Man*, but more pertinently in *The Simulacra* (1964), a Philip K Dick novel about a secret governing council which rules a totalitarian society using a simulacrum android President. Dick was as much an influence on Gallagher as Bester and Haldeman[48]. For example, *The World Jones Made* (1956), *The Minority Report* (1956), and *The Three Stigmata of Palmer Eldritch* (1964) feature 'precogs' who can see into the future, mutants who share a similar faculty with the Tharils in *Warriors' Gate*.

In Dick's *The Man in the High Castle* (1962), characters use the *I Ching*, known as the Oracle, to decide their own futures and enter the synchronic time between an alternate reality, where a post-War United States is divided between the Third Reich and Imperial Japan, and a reality where the Allies won the War. Dick also used the *I Ching* to decide the outcomes of narratives and characters, turning his novel into a metafictional, abstract text about free will,

---

[47] Kooijman, Jaap, *Fabricating the Absolute Fake: America in Contemporary Pop Culture*, p98-9.
[48] Morris, Jonathan, 'The Fact of Fiction: *Warriors' Gate*', DWM #499.

simultaneous realities and synchronicity[49]. Gallagher's own use of the *I Ching* in *Warriors' Gate* was inspired by a Granada colleague, who'd read about it in a women's magazine and encouraged him to try its powers of divination by tossing three coins and looking up their heads and tails configurations. He recalled: 'there's a certain magic in an oracle in that if you make it of the right proportion of specific and obscure then people will find in it something entirely relevant to them and entirely meaningful to them.'[50]

---

[49] Psychoanalyst Carl Jung (1875-1961) first described synchronicity in the publication of his 1928 seminars, *Dream Analysis*. He theorised that events are not only connected by causality but also through a series of meaningful coincidences, and he closely linked this theory to the *I Ching*. Jung's theories find some parity with Bohm's holistic view of the universe.
[50] **Toby Hadoke's Who's Round** #166.

CHAPTER 2: THE DREAM TIME

An Alternative to Suicide's success prompted director Martin Jenkins to forward the script in the BBC's internal mail to the **Doctor Who** office without Gallagher's knowledge. Gallagher was grateful to Jenkins 'because the next thing I knew was that I was getting a call from Christopher Bidmead asking if I'd be interested in writing for **Doctor Who**.'[51] Bidmead was 'impressed by the play's momentum'[52] and met Gallagher in December 1979. A number of ideas were discussed, including an unused one-page outline called 'The Dream Time'.

'The Dream Time' was an unused proposal, eventually replaced by **The Babylon Run**, to conclude Gallagher's radio trilogy and originated from a rough plan outlined in 1978 under the working title of 'Time Wars'. In it, the simulacrum of Randall becomes a renegade set on slave revolt. Gallagher's notion of a 'robot' slave class turning on its masters involved 'slipping sideways into alternative pasts + futures – army of simulacra/time-slice beings – finds a competing evil force and fights it'. On the back of a Granada pay packet envelope, a further note offers a setting of 'Earth's history changed + made barren – has been altered back in time not to develop **but** one area of past held rigid – so they still exist.'[53] These hint at what appears in 'The Dream Time's outline but they also prefigure elements of *Warriors' Gate*: the void, the mirrors, the robot Gundans

---

[51] Cook, 'In Space No-one Can Hear You Scream'.
[52] *Doctor Who: The Complete History*, Volume 33, p53.
[53] Hull Archives, UDGA **The Last Rose of Summer** file. Undated notes.

hunting down the Tharils, and the cyclic history of enslavement they recount in the banqueting hall.

The title 'The Dream Time' first appears in the working notes for **Hunters' Moon**, outlining character and plot beats about Randall. Simultaneously, it seems, an Australian colleague at Granada told Gallagher about the Aboriginal 'alcheringa' – 'the Dreamtime' or 'the Dreaming'. Anthropologists coined this as an umbrella term for a number of words that express the Aboriginal creation narratives, spiritual philosophy and worldview. In a belief system that dates back some 65,000 years, the 'Aboriginal concept of time is too subtle' to be described in Western terms and 'their understanding of the Dreaming appears to point to a conception of time as circular rather than linear.'[54] They are connected to their original ancestors, to the sacred lands, the plants and the creatures that inhabit them, within a continuum of the past, the present and the future, in a beginning that never ended. This has intriguing connections to the notion of inter-dimensional travel in 'The Dream Time'. Furthermore, in relation to *Warriors' Gate*, it reflects the use of Carl Jung's idea of the collective unconscious [55], the holistic, cyclic universe in Taoist philosophy and David Bohm's theory that Bidmead

---

[54] Edwards, William Howell, *An Introduction to Aboriginal Societies*, p17.

[55] Jung proposed that this is a level of the unconscious shared with other members of the human species, comprising latent memories from our ancestral and evolutionary past. In a 1936 lecture, he suggested that it 'does not develop individually but is inherited. It consists of pre-existent forms, the archetypes, which can only become conscious secondarily and which give definite form to certain psychic contents.'

alerted Gallagher to during the writing of the serial, proposing that the universe is a massive hologram, an interconnected consciousness, from which physical reality folds and unfolds.

'The Dream Time's one-page outline continues from **Hunters' Moon**'s conclusion, where the simulacra crew search for a planet to settle on. Mitchell, an imperfect simulacrum, is desperate for human company and escapes from their ship to explore a planet from which they have received messages. However, he steals a vital component of the navigation computer to force the crew to follow him. Despite the transmissions, the planet is a wasteland and the only remnant of an apparently lost civilisation is 'a deserted stasis chamber, fully equipped and still ready to receive visitors.' Randall tracks Mitchell to a transmitter mast and discovers they are not alone in their search. Another race has used Mitchell to trap them, and a battle triggers the opening of a gateway to an alien world. Mitchell 'slips through a series of gateways through a number of parallel worlds.' The outline continues:

> 'The culmination of this chase is at a major interchange of alternate gateways like a planetary hall of mirrors as Mitchell is chased by both Randall and a series of alternate-Randalls and aliens. A number of gateways are destroyed, but Mitchell finds the right one and closes it behind him… Closing of the gateway causes a rebound of the aliens' firepower.'[56]

Warriors' Gate's origins are more clearly demonstrated here. Mitchell's escape parallels Biroc absconding from the privateer to

---

[56] Hull Archives, UDGA *Warriors' Gate* (file 1). 'The Dream Time' undated outline.

bring the TARDIS to the void. Mitchell and Randall are versions of the Doctor and the Tharils and the alien threat becomes Rorvik and the slavers. Recalling the beings that slip sideways into alternate timelines in Gallagher's 'Time Wars' notes, the gateway as a hall of mirrors into the past and future and the aliens' rebounding blasts are also very recognisable elements of *Warriors' Gate*.

Using this outline Gallagher pitched a five-page narrative to Bidmead in which 'there was no E-Space, no K-9, and given that I didn't know how far ahead we were looking I referred not to Romana but to "the Doctor's current assistant". Adric was not, as yet, a part of the show.'[57] Various notes, which can be dated to January 1980, further define central ideas and motifs:

> 'The stasis chamber is a single room – the banquet hall? – in an old dark house – the house is the gateway & the rest of it is elsewhere – the runaway is dragged through, like the mirrors in *Orphée* – bring in the "Beauty & Beast" myth with the aliens and the assistant – she tames the beast. Beast is like a ghost wandering through the house, opting in and out of time as he looks for a lost something.'[58]

Gallagher establishes the banqueting hall and gateway of *Warriors' Gate* in relation to the influential work of French director Jean

---

[57] Gallagher, Stephen, 'Scripting *Warriors' Gate*: So what actually happened?' *In-Vision* #54, season 18 overview.
[58] Hull Archives, UDGA *Warriors' Gate* (file 1). Undated notes.

Cocteau and his films *La Belle et la Bête* (1946) and *Orphée* (1950)[59]. As Gallagher later acknowledged, *La Belle et la Bête*:

> '...formed the style of the whole thing: the look of the Tharils and the whole kind of magical environment, the haunted castle, were very much my tribute to that particular movie. The journey through the weird landscape owed a lot to *Orphée*, the other really influential Cocteau film.'[60]

Cocteau's *La Belle et la Bête* further influenced the March 1980 breakdown. Gallagher describes the cliffhanger to the first episode, where the Doctor, in search of Biroc in the 'castle', discovers an armoury 'lit, like the rest of the rooms, by candles that never burn down; it's as if they've been burning since the beginning of time.'[61]

A breakdown of four episodes complete with cliffhangers, derived from the five-page document, also describes how the hijacked TARDIS arrives at 'an ancient but disused interchange' in the 'ambivalent existence' between E-Space and N-Space. The Doctor and an unnamed assistant meet the 'bedraggled and disreputable' crew of the disabled warp ship. While the assistant concludes that the warp ship and crew are not as innocent as they seem, the Doctor

---

[59] Jean Cocteau (1889-1963) was a French poet, writer, designer, artist and filmmaker. He made his first film in 1925 and his last in 1960 and was regarded by the French 'New Wave' directors François Truffaut and Jean-Luc Godard as an auteur. His films integrate all aspects of his work – poetry, theatre, graphic design, sculpture, music, dance and choreography.

[60] Travers, Paul, 'Valley of Who', interview with Gallagher, DWM #139.

[61] Gallagher, 'Scripting *Warriors' Gate*'.

follows their missing navigator to the 'castle'. The first episode ends with the runaway ghostly time-sensitive menacing the Doctor.

Episode 2 sees the Doctor and the assistant uncover the true purposes of the interchange and the slave ship, after seeing a time-sensitive being revived. The Doctor escapes to the castle, when the crew threaten to make him their navigator, and falls through a 'mirror like door'. The maze-like house on the other side of the mirror is the focus of episode 3. The assistant and a revived time-sensitive also escape and the Captain of the ship decides 'to blast open the gateway.' The final episode explains 'the independent action of the navigator' as the means of bringing the Doctor to the void to help free the other slaves. They survive the destruction of the slave ship because the navigator puts 'each of his fellows out of phase.' The Doctor's problem of being lost in E-Space remains unresolved at this stage[62].

The undated note 'Dr Who meeting 2' covered Gallagher's next meeting with Bidmead to develop and strengthen the characters and the plot. He was briefed about Adric, the departures of K-9 and Romana, and the E-Space trilogy concluding with the Doctor's 'emergence from the "anti-matter universe".' The void between overlapping universes and its old house or castle was considered a 'halfway house as a means thru?'[63] As Gallagher later recalled:

> 'The principle behind the season was [that] the TARDIS had
> to be got out of E-Space. I fastened on the idea of, "Well,

---

[62] Hull Archives, UDGA *Warriors' Gate* (file 2). 'The Dream Time' episode breakdown.

[63] Hull Archives, UDGA *Warriors' Gate* (file 1). 'Dr Who meeting 2' undated note.

what's between E-Space and ordinary space?" There must be a point you're moving from negative numbers into positive numbers. There must be a kind of tipping point where nothing exists – it's neither one nor the other. So, my notion of the void between the two spaces was that, and the idea that there could be various things trapped in the void.'[64]

The gateway, an old house bridging the interchange, would become Romana's TARDIS and her way of travelling through the E-Space universe with K-9, whose functions, damaged from the time winds when the TARDIS was hijacked, were restored by crossing through the mirrors[65]. Gallagher's meeting established the major elements of the story: 'the slave ship for time-sensitives, the dusty castle in a strange void, the mirrors and the time winds, the initial hijacking of the TARDIS, the final mass escape.'[66] Other memorable motifs, such as 'coin-tossing as means of navigation' and the Doctor 'working out an *I Ching* based on the last few journeys' were also noted down at this stage[67]. Rather like Dick, Gallagher applied *I Ching* principles to assemble the plot's disparate elements and 'all those kind of things swirled together and out of that came really just a one-pager where I just broke it down into four separate little episodes, and that one-pager really was the map for the whole thing.'[68]

After their 30 January meeting Gallagher wrote to Bidmead about 'refocussing the story so that the Doctor becomes of more central

---

[64] **Toby Hadoke's Who's Round** #166.
[65] Hull Archives, UDGA *Warriors' Gate* (file 1). Undated notes.
[66] Gallagher, 'Scripting *Warriors' Gate*'.
[67] Hull Archives, UDGA *Warriors' Gate* (file 1). Undated notes.
[68] **Toby Hadoke's Who's Round** #166.

importance', realising the setting in 'practical production terms with regard to the required sets' and changing the cliffhanger to the first episode 'so that the potential menace of the time-sensitive navigator remains intact.'

Gallagher's letter also explains the warp ship's arrival in the void: 'Like negative numbering, the continuum exists outside of observable phenomena as a necessary half-step in a calculation – except the warp ship is unable to complete the step.' The crew deliberately allows the navigator to escape, ride the time winds, and lead them to the TARDIS to find a Time Lord who can repair their warp drive. Gallagher makes the Doctor a more active participant by becoming embroiled in the Captain's plans. This is particularly relevant to the philosophy behind the story when, after he and one of the time-sensitives escape to prevent the Captain from blasting the gateway, the Doctor realises these events are synchronous and the navigator has planned this to free the other slaves by taking them out of phase during the back-blast. Intriguingly, Gallagher also concludes 'the Captain and his crew aren't killed by the back-blast from the gateway -- they are simply drawn into it and stranded there as wandering ghosts, bickering as before.'

He describes the void as a place where matter 'is simply passing through' except for the structure of the gateway. All details and objects are 'wrapped into a white fog.' Vehicles orientate themselves by their relative positions to each other. The slaver ship uses mass detectors whereas the Doctor employs a 'more elegant method of navigation.' Gallagher describes this as:

> 'the Taoist theory that every element of the universe somehow implies the existence of every other element, and

that the behaviour of one implies the behaviour of every other – the basis of most fortune-telling methods from astrology to the *I Ching* – the Doctor's method is to toss a coin and mentally ask it which way to go.'

Gallagher also changes the climax of the first episode. He abandons the threat of the ghostly time-sensitive and instead opts for a chamber filled with 'vaguely medieval' battle-armour where the Doctor examines a silver globe, 'a temporal distortion bomb' made from the same substance as the mirrors, that provides a clue about the nature of the gateway. However, unseen by him, one of the suits of armour reactivates to attack him[69].

After Gallagher completed his episode schematics, now including Adric, Romana and K-9, Bidmead wrote back, updating him about the elements that the season intended to address. Given that Lalla Ward mutually agreed with Nathan-Turner in the New Year that she would leave during the season, Bidmead refers to Romana refusing the summons back to Gallifrey, the relationship between her and the Doctor ending with her as 'his equivalent in E-Space' and accepting his parting gift of K-9. He interprets the nature of the CVEs that the TARDIS fell through into E-Space, and suggests that the way out is difficult because 'theoretically at least an almost infinite (and almost infinitely improbable) regression of charged vacuums can be nested inside each other like Chinese boxes.'[70] There's a scene in Gallagher's

---

[69] Hull Archives, UDGA *Warriors' Gate* (file 1). Letter to Bidmead, 5 February 1980.
[70] Hull Archives, UDGA *Warriors' Gate* (file 1). Letter from Bidmead, 15 March 1980.

schematic of episode 3 where the time-sensitive navigator demonstrates the nature of the gateway in a 'sequence showing infinity of rooms.'[71] It's a cinematic visual, hinting at the narrative's melting pot of ideas, including Taoist connectedness and Bohm's theory of the implicate order of the universe. It also foreshadows the recursion that Bidmead introduced in *Logopolis* and *Castrovalva*.

A 25-page scene breakdown, commissioned on 17 March, was received on 27 March and featured the E-Space setting, Adric, Romana and K-9, and covered many aspects of Bidmead's letter. Each episode was broken down and covered by eight pages of numbered scenes and cliffhangers. In Gallagher's schematics the time-sensitive characters were named Biroc and Laszlo (after cinematographers Joseph Biroc, who worked with director Robert Aldrich, and Ernest Laszlo, who shot Robert Aldrich's film noir *Kiss Me Deadly* (1955), one of several films that director Paul Joyce later screened to the production team to propose his visual sense of *Warriors' Gate*). The privateer's crew were unnamed but a separate undated note lists them: Rorvik, Packard, Sagan, Lane and 'old men' Aldo and Waldo. Gallagher named Rorvik after American science journalist and novelist David Rorvik, who 'had written a bogus account of human cloning that I'd read in the research for *Chimera*, and I took [...] his name.'[72] Cosmologist Carl Sagan was the origin of the privateer's namesake.

---

[71] Hull Archives, UDGA *Warriors' Gate* (file 1). Undated episode schematics.

[72] Gallagher, email to author. He is referring to the controversial 1978 book *In His Image: The Cloning of a Man* in which Rorvik claims to have been part of a project to successfully clone a human being.

While Gallagher completed the breakdown, Bidmead worked with Christopher Priest to pull 'Sealed Orders' into shape. A time-paradox political thriller set on Gallifrey, it featured multiple TARDISes and a duplicate Doctor. After receiving the scripts, Bidmead recalled:

> 'I can't exactly remember what went wrong. The first draft was a very good story, but showed lack of TV experience. I think I made the mistake of overestimating the amount of time I'd have to work side-by-side with Chris...'[73]

Priest was very unhappy with the changes to the brief he was asked to incorporate and Bidmead's rewriting and editing of his scripts. According to Bidmead, Priest had 'too much of the novelist's self-esteem and sensibility to want his stuff kicked around by this hack to make it work, so we had some, shall we say, creative tensions!'[74] Priest withdrew and eventually 'Sealed Orders' was abandoned[75]. Gallagher, knowing Priest was commissioned before him, was uneasy:

The book was the subject of a defamation suit by a British scientist whose thesis and name had been used without his permission. The book was ruled to be a hoax despite Rorvik's claims to the contrary. Mitchell is renamed 'Rorvik' in Gallagher's *Dying of Paradise*.

[73] Anghelides, Peter, 'Signed, Sealed, Delivered, Discarded', *In-Vision* #54.

[74] Griffiths, 'Fifth Man In'.

[75] Unfortunately, Priest's commission for another four-part serial 'The Enemy Within' in 1981 ended with Priest not only lodging a formal complaint with the Writers' Guild, about payment and Nathan-Turner and script editor Eric Saward's handling of the commission, but also an apology from David Reid, Head of Series and Serials.

'It made the whole thing feel a bit like a horse race. I can't imagine someone of Chris Priest's calibre stumbling at the quality hurdle – I suspect it may have had more to do with Chris being a bloody good science fiction writer who wouldn't compromise much to accommodate the format of the show.'[76]

To that end, four episodes of 'The Dream Time' were commissioned on 14 April and, after further meetings in May, Gallagher delivered the first drafts on 11 June, accepted by Nathan-Turner and Bidmead on 30 June subject to rewrites. The drafts incorporated very detailed mise-en-scène, were not arranged in standard numbered scenes and used asterisks to denote scene changes. Gallagher later acknowledged:

'...let me be the first to concede that you couldn't take them onto the studio floor as they stood. My lack of TV experience had led to their having dialogue like a radio play and stage directions with the density of novel description. TV scripts are, as anyone who's seen one will know, bare and schematic documents more akin to blueprints. Mine weren't.'[77]

In Gallagher's first drafts, the time-sensitives are called the Caliban. This is one of several Shakespearean references and alludes to Caliban, an island native who is a bitter and reluctant servant to the exiled magician Prospero in *The Tempest* (1611). The supernatural offspring of the witch Sycorax, he is a base counterpoint to Prospero's other unearthly servant, the spiritual Ariel. Modern

---

[76] Freeman, John, 'The Man in the Control Seat', interview with Gallagher, *In-Vision* #50, *Warriors' Gate*.
[77] Gallagher, 'Scripting *Warriors' Gate*'.

commentators see *The Tempest* as a parable of colonialism and imperialism and an exploration of the master-servant relationship, where both Caliban and Ariel are Prospero's property. Although they desire their freedom, they labour under a power Prospero wields through physical and psychological suffering and oppression. It's interesting that Gallagher chose to name his enslaved former imperialists after Caliban, the ambiguous noble savage usurped from the island by Prospero. Betrayed by his fellow slave Ariel, he is willing to serve new masters Trinculo and Stephano, who might be kinder in their treatment and give him his freedom. However, the magical Ariel is just as much a slave under Prospero's command and, more akin to the Tharils of *Warriors' Gate*, a spirit of fire and air capable of manipulating the forces of nature.

This literary allusion is lost when later drafts of 'The Dream Time' and *Warriors' Gate* rename the Calibans as Tharks (Packard also describes Biroc as a 'Thark with a Thoat's head' in Gallagher's first drafts), Tharls and, finally, Tharils in the camera scripts[78]. Yet, the themes about corrupt command structures, abuse of power and slavery remain. The cycle of master-slave relationships between the once powerful Calibans and the human slavers returns to a recurring theme in Gallagher's earlier work. They are another manifestation of the various humans, clones and simulacra wanting freedom from oppressive, technologised societies and corporations. Where the conditioned Spacers were put to work running the Company ships in *An Alternative to Suicide*, the Tharils in *Warriors' Gate* are not only

---

[78] A Thoat is an eight-legged Martian riding beast and a Thark is a fierce, 15-foot-tall green Martian warrior. Both are references to Edgar Rice Burroughs' **Barsoom** stories which begin with *A Princess of Mars*, first serialised in 1912.

kept subdued and put in dwarf star alloy irons by the human slavers but are also, through biotechnology, violently forced to visualise and navigate the ship's warp jumps. Essentially, these ex-colonialists work for their former slaves as flesh and blood versions of the *I Ching*.

Gallagher expanded this in his second draft of episode 1, with an opening scene showing the privateer running an anti-slavery blockade and sustaining damage from an Antonine Killer missile before jumping to light speed. Although it was dropped from the script, the restored scene in the novelisation describes the pilot's perspective: 'Four privateers had tried to run the blockade, all four of them wiped out by the Antonine Killers, the Brotherhood, the clan. The anti-slavery alliance could be fun, as long as you didn't take it too seriously.'[79]

In Gallagher's pseudonymous novelisation, Biroc also describes the conditions aboard the privateer and reflects upon the Tharils' history at the gateway:

> 'Hundreds, maybe even thousands, of his own people, stacked tight like cards in a deck and drugged into a placid sleep by the life support systems, feed tubes and pumps that barely sustained life, in conditions that otherwise would kill more than half their number.'[80]

> 'Biroc stood in the gloom of the hall, and looked on the lost glory of the Tharils. He knew that he was in the middle of a legend, but it was a legend of defeat – no more than an echo

---

[79] Lydecker, John, *Doctor Who and Warriors' Gate*, p5.
[80] Lydecker, *Warriors' Gate*, p19.

of the greatness that had preceded the enslavement of the race, the fall which had scattered them throughout a thousand systems to live as land-grubbing beggars while they waited for the hunters to drop from the sky.'[81]

The Antonine Killer sequence possibly alludes to the blockades of Africa when the United Kingdom, having passed the Slave Trade Act of 1807, established the West Africa Squadron of Royal Navy ships in 1808 to patrol the coast and intercept and search any ships suspected of carrying slaves. The lengthy opening to episode 1, showing the Tharils imprisoned in the ship's hold, also visually 'draws on imagery of 18th Century slave ships familiar from the 1977 American mini-series, **Roots**.'[82]

Gallagher, consistent with his radio work, is concerned with the exchanges of power and the mechanisms of oppression. The Calibans were once lords of an empire that enslaved humanity, until they developed the robot Shoguns (renamed in further drafts as 'Gun' and, finally, as 'Gundans') to withstand the corrosive effects of the time winds and pursue their masters through the gateway. In the novelisation, the Doctor contemplates how both the Tharils and the slavers were in a position similar to Caliban and Ariel, attempting to regain their status by defying their master Prospero: 'Yes, the Doctor thought, the weak did indeed enslave themselves; by setting themselves up as unjust masters they handed out invitations to rebellion and revenge.'[83]

---

[81] Lydecker, *Warriors' Gate*, p46.
[82] Wiggins, Martin, *Warriors' Gate* DVD production text, episode 1.
[83] Lydecker, *Warriors' Gate*, p105.

While the narrative themes and visual elements of what would become *Warriors' Gate* are clearly present, Gallagher's first drafts appear to be funnier than the rehearsal scripts. He gives the crew of the rickety privateer much witty interplay and squeezes more cynicism out of Rorvik's frustrations with their incompetence. Aldo and Waldo are berated in episode 1 for bursting onto the bridge to empty the rubbish bins and their retort 'we slave for the likes of you' is a particularly self-reflexive line[84]. There's some physical, **Keystone Kops**-style slapstick in episode 2 when three crewmen end up in a heap chasing after the Doctor's reflection in the banqueting hall mirrors. Adric and K-9 also share many more scenes and the effects of the time wind damage on the robot dog, as he randomly spews poetry and songs, swing bathetically between the sublime and the ridiculous. However, this humour was toned down, particularly when Barry Letts cautioned that even in the rehearsal scripts it should be 'played absolutely for real (letting the comedy be 'real' too).'[85]

Gallagher's very descriptive camera positions, presenting viewpoints from behind these mirrors, make it into the finished episodes and anticipate elements of Joyce's film sensibility. Significantly, episode 3 beautifully describes the Doctor's first visit to the gardens on the other side of the mirror.

> 'He's keyed into a black-and-white still of a formal garden, Versailles style; in the distance the palatial house can be seen.

---

[84] Hull Archives, UDGA *Warriors' Gate* (file 2). Gallagher, 'The Dream Time', episode 1, p19.

[85] BBC Written Archives Centre (WAC) file T65/256/1, *Warriors' Gate*. Barry Letts, Notes, 29 August 1980.

But the still has been retouched; the sky is a pink watercolour wash, and the house is in ruins. The greenery and stonework all appear to have been dusted with a light frost.

'There's nobody to be seen, but there are the sounds of a light-hearted garden party nearby, the two versions of reality jarring together.'[86]

However, speaking to *In-Vision* in 1994, Joyce appeared to lay claim to this imagery:

'The other thing which they'd never really seen done before was the way I used black-and-white photographs. I had a notion that when they got to this particular place beyond the gateway, it would look something like Powis Castle. I thought that a way of playing with this idea of everything being real but unreal would be to have people in full colour moving through a black-and-white environment.'[87]

In *In-Vision*'s overview of season 18, an unhappy Gallagher confirmed, with the first draft scripts as evidence, that this was originally his idea. Even if we give Joyce the benefit of hindsight, that in trying to explain how he achieved this image technically he might have mistakenly claimed it as his idea, the Doctor and Romana keyed in against a monochrome image of formal gardens featured in the first drafts written before Joyce joined the production.

---

[86] Hull Archives. Gallagher, 'The Dream Time', episode 3, p13.
[87] Newman, Philip, 'Joyce Words', interview with Joyce, *In-Vision* #50.

In episode 4, Rorvik's strategy, of using the ship's back-blast to break through the gateway, is retained from Gallagher's original 'Dream Time' outline, and includes Rorvik's much quoted line: 'I want a landing that wouldn't ripple the skin on a custard.'[88] The Doctor and Laszlo set off to sabotage the back-blast and in this draft, amusingly, become the targets of Rorvik's rant at Aldo and Waldo who, once again, disrupt the bridge with their insistence on emptying the bins. Gallagher also has Sagan and Lane, playing cards down in the hold, openly mock Rorvik. The central premise, of precognition determining action or inaction, is present and underlined when the Doctor realises Biroc is also on board and can 'let himself slide out of phase' to avoid the back-blast and simultaneously rescue the captured Calibans by taking them out of phase as well. The Doctor informs Laszlo that Biroc has known about the back-blast all along: 'He wanted it to happen, and that's why he waited and did nothing! The blast won't harm your people, it will free them!'[89] Finally, Romana takes the TARDIS a few minutes into the future to avoid the back-blast and witnesses Biroc leading 'a line of Calibans all shimmering [...] like Banquo with the parade of kings' out of the wreckage of the privateer[90]. This climax is slightly different and, per Gallagher's letter to Bidmead in February, also features the ghostly and blackened survivors of the destroyed privateer being beckoned into the ruins of the gateway by one of the Shogun robots.

---

[88] Hull Archives. Gallagher, 'The Dream Time', episode 4, p7.
[89] Hull Archives. Gallagher, 'The Dream Time', episode 4, p22.
[90] Hull Archives. Gallagher, 'The Dream Time', episode 4, p24.

CHAPTER 3: ALDO AND WALDO

On 20 June 1980 Nathan-Turner requested that director Paul Joyce be engaged to direct **Doctor Who**. David Rose, the Head of English Regions Drama based at BBC Birmingham, had recommended Joyce. Nathan-Turner, keen to use aspiring writers and directors on his first season of **Doctor Who**, should be acknowledged for supporting inexperienced directors such as Joyce and Lovett Bickford[91] rather than relying on a pool of journeyman television directors. Only later was Joyce, like Bickford, regarded as a contentious choice, certainly by BBC management in the production's aftermath, but his work on *Warriors' Gate* transformed it into a singular and original piece of television.

Well known for his documentaries on filmmakers, actors and artists made by his company Lucida Productions, Joyce's wider career spanned theatre, film, television drama, documentary, photography, painting and writing. In 1965, after two terms at The London School of Film Technique, he had used his final grant cheque to fund his first film *The Goad*, an adaptation of Samuel Beckett's short mime play *Act Without Words II*, which he'd seen during an experimental programme of five short plays, *Expeditions One*, at the Aldwych Theatre in July 1964. He saw the play as a meditation on the relentless rituals of modern life, the empty passage of time 'from birth to death presented in the simplest of terms. (Two sacks, each containing first, a dozy human, and secondly, a spruce, athletic one, are prodded progressively across the stage by a sharp metal object

---

[91] Bickford directed *The Leisure Hive* (1980), the opening story of the season and it was, like *Warriors' Gate*, a difficult birth.

on wheels, "The Goad").' [92] Perhaps he saw that sense of relentlessness when he encountered the world of Rorvik and his crew in *Warriors' Gate*. He also fastened onto one of Beckett's recurring themes: rubbish. 'Beckett's identification of miscellaneous rubbish with the world, minds and bodies of his characters indicates its importance in his writing,' and it was a signifier of mortality and the modern world in many of his novels, theatre and radio plays. The tramps in his breakthrough play *Waiting for Godot* (1953) also inhabit a world of 'hand-me downs, cast-offs and detritus' where ritual and habit are bound up with change brought about by uncertainty[93]. Again, the rundown privateer is a tangible evocation of Beckett. Joyce's work continued to incorporate elements of the absurd and surreal, a sensibility that he would detect in Gallagher's scripts for *Warriors' Gate*. This could perhaps be traced back to a formative moment in his childhood, when he saw a black-and-white film that was:

> '...a bit like that Laurel and Hardy one where they have difficulty getting a piano up the stairs [...] only it was the delivery of a stereo or a radiogram, of enormous proportions, which was taken upstairs and delivered to a bachelor in his apartment. It was what he'd always been wanting, he plugs it in, twiddles around with it, listens to the music. Magnificent. Then he thinks it's time for a bite and he goes to switch it off. Switches it off and the music continues. Hits the thing. And

---

[92] Joyce, 'Guinness with Godot', unpublished essay emailed to author, 20 April 2018.
[93] Bates, Julie, *Beckett's Art of Salvage: Writing and Material Imagination, 1932-1987*, pp6-9.

the fucking thing won't stop. In the end, he smashes it to a pulp. How about that for a surreal situation? That gave me film and a Beckett kind of situation.'[94]

in 1966 Joyce saw *A Separate Peace*, an interlinked play and documentary in the BBC Two series **Double Image**, written by Tom Stoppard[95] and, always on the look out for interesting writers to work with, he wrote to him at the BBC. They met and discussed Stoppard's plan to develop a film from his 15-minute radio play *The Dissolution of Dominic Boot* (1963). Stoppard's work, along with Beckett's, appealed to Joyce's dark sense of humour. *Dominic Boot* is a rapidly paced farce that follows Dominic as he travels in a taxi to try and raise the money for his ever-growing fare from various banks, his firm's petty cash, and by raiding the gas meter. He gives his possessions, including the engagement ring he bought for his prospective fiancée, to the taxi driver in exchange for the fare and is left with nothing but his pyjamas and a raincoat. It stretches a mundane situation – paying for a taxi – to absurd lengths. When

---

[94] Joyce, interview with author. Our efforts to identify this film have been unsuccessful.

[95] Tom Stoppard is a prolific writer working in radio, theatre, television and film. He came to prominence with the play *Rosencrantz and Guildenstern Are Dead* (1967) and has since enjoyed a successful stage career. As noted in Nigel Farndale's 2010 *Telegraph* interview, his work deals with 'philosophical concepts in a witty, ironic and linguistically complex way, usually with multiple timelines and visual humour.' *Arcadia*, for example, is essentially a country-house comedy. However, inspired by James Gleick's book *Chaos: Making a New Science* (1987), it also forges connections with thermodynamics and the dichotomies between past and present, order and chaos, certainty and uncertainty.

Stoppard's *Rosencrantz and Guildenstern Are Dead* became a huge success in 1967, Joyce expected *Dominic Boot* to be abandoned, but Stoppard kept his word and, with Joyce, developed the radio script into the short film *The Engagement* (1970). *Rosencrantz and Guildenstern Are Dead*, Stoppard's breakthrough play, is of great relevance to *Warriors' Gate*. An alternative perspective on Shakespeare's *Hamlet* (1603), it's told from the viewpoint of two minor characters, Rosencrantz and Guildenstern, summoned by King Claudius to snap the moody Dane out of his melancholia. In *Hamlet*, Claudius sends them to accompany Hamlet by sea to England, carrying a letter that, on arrival, orders Hamlet's execution. Unbeknownst to them, Hamlet has rewritten the letter, instructing the executioner instead to kill them. Hamlet escapes a pirate attack on their ship and their deaths are reported later in the play.

Stoppard's existential comedy exploits the convention in *Hamlet* that the two characters are inseparable. In Stoppard's play they are often mistaken for one another, refer to each other by the wrong names and doubt their own identities as they progress inevitably to their fate. Rosencrantz and Guildenstern are often compared to Vladimir and Estragon, *Waiting for Godot*'s absurdist, ruminating comedic tramps where, as Kenneth Tynan observed of Stoppard's characters, 'the sight of two bewildered men playing pointless games in a theatrical void while the real action unfolds off stage inevitably recalls Beckett.' [96] They hurtle towards their destiny 'passing the time in a place without any visible character', which is

---

[96] Quoted in Duncan, Joseph E, 'Godot Comes: *Rosencrantz and Guildenstern Are Dead'. Ariel Vol 12, No 4* (October 1981), pp57-58.

also a good description of the privateer's crew trapped in the white void of *Warriors' Gate*[97].

Gallagher evokes Rosencrantz and Guildenstern and Vladimir and Estragon in the characters of Aldo and Waldo, originally described as 'two small and skinny old men who are always seen dragging a half-filled black plastic bag around.' Their names are almost identical; thus they are easily confused for one another and, tramp-like in demeanour, they wear tatty, hastily repaired oversized spacesuits[98]. They irritate the crew and provide a comedic Greek chorus to the events on the privateer[99]. In an amusing scene dropped from the later drafts, Lane interrogates them about what happens to their rubbish collections. Once collected, they redistribute it around the ship, thereby securing their jobs in perpetuity and, most importantly, refuse to dump it into space because 'That's unhygienic!'[100] Joyce clearly recognised the Beckettian qualities in Aldo and Waldo whom, coincidentally, Gallagher based on the cleaners at Granada:

> 'Two women who would come breezing into the control room in the middle of the most complicated commercial break that you ever had to operate, shouting at the top of their voices,

---

[97] Stoppard, Tom, *Rosencrantz and Guildenstern Are Dead*, stage directions Act I, p1.

[98] Hull Archives. Gallagher, 'The Dream Time', episode 1, p16.

[99] BBC WAC file T65/256/1. Letts, 29 August 1980. Waldo and Aldo were renamed Royce and Aldo when Letts' cautioned that, in using them as comedic figures, 'Waldo and Aldo in particular [shouldn't] regress to the very facetiousness we so disliked in the past. Immediately the thing becomes a silly pantomime instead of "real" science fiction.'

[100] Hull Archives. Gallagher, 'The Dream Time', episode 2, p24.

"Bins, bins, come on give us your bins!" They had no awareness of anything else that was going on. And you realised that there was no point saying to them, "Could you just wait for a moment?" "Oh no, we've got to have your bins." It was easier just to give them the bins and get them out of there as quickly as possible so you could get on with work that was actually appearing before the eyeballs of about 12,000,000 people at that moment.'

The hierarchies within the privateer crew, their relationship with Rorvik, and moreover, Biroc's enforced duties as navigator, reflect an oppressive situation where Gallagher 'was surrounded by engineers who had worked in Granada for like 20 years or so and had no respect for the management whatsoever.' [101] When Nathan-Turner discussed the scripts with Gallagher, he understood 'that this whole setup – the spaceship with people who were just there to earn a living – was actually his appreciation of Granada Television.' [102] Gallagher also recalled Bidmead's perspective:

'He could see the image of the Tharil chained to the chair with its limited amount of movement as a metaphor for me in the bowels of Granada TV, controlling the station and desperate to break out into the wide world beyond. It was a very perceptive thought, and I was probably the last one to see it at the time.' [103]

---

[101] **Toby Hadoke's Who's Round** #166.

[102] Tulloch, John, and Manuel Alvarado, *Doctor Who: The Unfolding Text*, p175.

[103] Freeman, 'The Man in the Control Seat'.

This blend of gritty science fiction and observational comedy was not lost on Joyce, who wanted 'to deal with universal themes and human frailty and the ability for people to laugh'[104], and appreciated the echoes of Stoppard and Beckett captured in the mundane lives of the privateer crew. Like Vladimir and Estragon or Rosencrantz and Guildenstern, they navigate an uncertain universe that they're too cynical, bored or oppressed to understand but they always have time for a spot of lunch, card games, betting, and routine insubordination.

Joyce believed that Beckett was essentially comedic in nature and:

> '...part of [...] a Shakespearean theatrical tradition, which had to do with banter, with passing time. How do you pass time? How did they pass time on a spaceship? There's fuck all to do. Check a few instruments and look after a few apparently dead bodies. Got hours and days to go. They smoke and play cards and bet on things.'

Gallagher made Aldo and Waldo a focus for comedy and often the object of Rorvik's ire, but a number of their funniest scenes were dropped from the rehearsal scripts. Joyce gave them new scenes in the rehearsal scripts because he felt:

> '[The] comedy of life, of peculiarities of human behaviour are the things that great directors pick up on. I'm not part of that but I just learn from it, as that's what I love, watching it, seeing it. So those things between the two characters, you know [...] it's *Rosencrantz and Guildenstern Are Dead*. It's *Waiting for Godot*.'[105]

---

[104] Joyce, interview with author.
[105] **Toby Hadoke's Who's Round** #167, 'Paul Joyce Part 2'.

There are several examples of Joyce's approach in the rehearsal scripts. In episode 1, Aldo and Waldo bet on whether Biroc survives the energy surge from a high-tension cable and they fuss about a lost storeroom key. After the privateer lands in the void, they observe à la Rozencrantz and Guildenstern that they are 'back in nowhere. Nowhere's somewhere. Somewhere that isn't even supposed to exist.' They banter about Rorvik and Romana, decline Rorvik's invitation to join an expedition to the gateway after Waldo excuses himself because 'the string in me leg's gone again', and choose which Thark to revive with the flip of a coin in episode 2. Both Rorvik and Sagan mistake Aldo and Waldo for each other (an in-joke that makes less sense after the characters names were changed and the idea of casting two actors similar in appearance was abandoned), they hide under the table during the lunch in the banqueting hall (another of Joyce's suggestions to Gallagher that was eventually cut from episode 3), and in episode 4 they convince themselves that Rorvik knows what he's doing with the MZ laser weapon until there's a huge explosion from the hall. They feign illness when Sagan comes to help them revive the Tharks and, as they hear the screams from inside the storage hold, Waldo concludes that 'It'll all end in tears, mark my words.'[106]

Rosencrantz and Guildenstern's opening, where the characters contemplate the nature of causality, probability and free will by betting on the outcomes of tossing coins, is a constant reference in *Warriors' Gate*. The Doctor proposes that tossing a coin might guide them out of E-Space, Adric uses a coin to navigate the void, and Aldo and Waldo use one to bet on Biroc's survival in the rehearsal script.

---

[106] *Warriors' Gate* rehearsal scripts.

That their coin freezes in mid toss as the privateer hits a time rift reflects Guildenstern's observation, of their spinning coins constantly turning heads up 90 times in a row, that 'Time has stopped dead.'[107]

Rather like Bidmead, Stoppard consciously explores theoretical science in his work, and *Rosencrantz and Guildenstern* was indicative of the quantum and chaos theory conundrums later and more explicitly explored in plays like *Hapgood* (1988)[108] and *Arcadia* (1993). After entering a void where subjectivity is constantly questioned and events are determined from seemingly random choices, Guildenstern observes, 'we can move, of course, change direction, rattle about but our movement is contained within a larger one that carries us along as inexorably as the wind or current.'[109] Guildenstern's observation that they are individuals being carried along by much larger, unseen currents reflects the influence of Bohm's implicate order theory on *Warriors' Gate*, where he proposed space and time emanated from an endlessly folding and unfolding multidimensional reality and within it there existed independent physical elements and human entities with relative autonomy[110].

---

[107] Stoppard, *Rosencrantz and Guildenstern Are Dead,* Act I, p6.

[108] *Hapgood* is a spy thriller that combines espionage with the non-determinism of quantum physics to explore free will and the conscious mind, causality and identity.

[109] Stoppard, *Rosencrantz and Guildenstern Are Dead,* Act III, p114.

[110] Storoy, David, 'David Bohm, Implicate Order and Holomovement'.

Stoppard's two characters are caught in a deterministic universe and 'they do nothing to help their friend Hamlet when they discover they carry a letter ordering his execution and they do nothing when they read the letter that Hamlet has swapped. They read their own death warrants and go to the gallows befuddled but without resistance.'[111] Waiting in *Hamlet*'s wings, they catch up with the play's tragic and inevitable events, just as:

> 'Biroc had managed to glimpse as a unity the events that would follow if the privateer and the TARDIS were brought together at the gateway. There had been no randomness in his actions, and no indecision in his failures to act. When Biroc watched and did nothing, it was because he already knew what was ahead.'[112]

In 1973, Joyce began an unfinished adaptation of Thomas Hinde's thriller *The Day the Call Came* (1964), written by fellow cineaste and Dulwich College alumnus Paul Mayersberg. The book's ambiguous narrative about paranoid schizophrenia may well have influenced Joyce later when he came to write and direct *Keep Smiling*, the **Play for Today** (1970-84) seen by Nathan-Turner in 1980. Joyce confirmed that the unfinished film was:

> '...a psychological study and there's something which is in the nature of film which absolutely accords with psychological states, and I don't think a lot of people quite realise that.'[113]

---

[111] Demastes, William, *The Cambridge Introduction to Tom Stoppard*, pp52-53.
[112] Lydecker, *Warriors' Gate*, p115.
[113] Joyce, interview with author.

His interest in psychological states may have drawn him to Rorvik, the equally frustrated and increasingly paranoid captain of the privateer in Gallagher's scripts.

Keep Smiling was commissioned in early 1979 by David Rose, whose work at BBC Birmingham for **Play for Today** had already caught Joyce's attention:

> 'One month, during three Wednesdays, three plays, fantastic plays, one *Red Shift* by Alan Garner and a couple of others, went out. It kept saying David Rose. I thought, fuck me, you know, he's a genius. [...] So I just wrote to him and said, look, your name seems to be on the most interesting stuff that I'm watching on BBC. So, he said come up.'[114]

Rose's track record as a producer spoke for itself and he was, primarily, a 'firm believer in the authority of the writer in the creation of original drama.'[115] At the time, plays and series were still being made as hybrids of studio-based interior sequences, focusing on characters and dialogue, and film inserts shot on location, providing verisimilitude and realism. Expressing regional identities in new and unusual ways in his plays, Rose worked with regional writers, many of whom were new to television, encouraged experimentation in the studio, and increased the number of plays made entirely on film that were, as Rose advocated, about

---

[114] **Toby Hadoke's Who's Round #165.**
[115] Cooke, Lez, *A Sense of Place: Regional British television drama, 1956-82*, p110.

'narrowing the gap between films and television.'[116] The esprit de corps at BBC Birmingham was described by writer David Hare as 'David Rose letting people do what they wanted and nobody in London knowing what was going on.'[117]

When Rose raised the issue of who was going to direct the play, Joyce offered a solution:

> 'So, I said, "I'm a director" and showed him [*The Engagement*]. And he liked that. So, he said, "Well, you know this is a 90-minute play and an hour will be recorded in the studio over three days and it'll be a half hour on 16mm film." So, I said, "That's fine." He said, "Well, what about studio? You haven't directed in the studio." So, I said, "Look, let me come and watch." And Mike Newell was directing then. So, I said, "let me ask kindly of the director to observe rehearsals and then the taping", you know.'[118]

Joyce recalled observing two days of rehearsals for *Solid Geometry*, a play adapted by Ian McEwan from his own short story, and either a producer's run or a technical run-through prior to recording. However, Head of Drama Shaun Sutton notified Rose, the director, producer and writer on 20 March that *Solid Geometry* was cancelled[119]. Its makers believed the BBC had banned the play and

---

[116] Young, Graham, 'David Rose talks of his time with BBC Birmingham at Pebble Mill,' *Birmingham Post*.

[117] Quoted in Kelly, Richard, ed, *Alan Clarke*, p69.

[118] **Toby Hadoke's Who's Round** #165.

[119] BBC WAC file T62/6/1, *Solid Geometry*. 'A Statement by the Makers' document, late March 1979. The cancellation of the play

according to McEwan, 'Stephen Gilbert, the producer, was sacked after publicly criticising the ban. He was reinstated after a union-backed appeal but with severely reduced responsibilities.'[120]

Therefore, Joyce was unable to experience the entire studio production routine and did not shadow Mike Newell's direction of the recording. He informed Rose that he had seen enough in rehearsals to 'know what to do. I don't need to see any more.'[121] *Keep Smiling* was made on the standard BBC production schedule: location film and rehearsals with the actors prior to studio, camera rehearsals and line-ups in studio in the morning and afternoon, rehearse-record from the afternoon to 10.00 pm in the evenings, and then several days of post-production. Joyce completed location filming first and rehearsed prior to studio recording scheduled between 15 and 18 September. The last of those dates was a four-hour studio-only session to complete the video electronic effects the play required. It was then edited and dubbed over four days in October.

---

became a bone of contention with the Writers' Guild and the ACTT union during a difficult period for BBC drama. Rose advised caution from the outset but, having had their fingers burnt with the banning of **Play for Today** productions *Brimstone and Treacle* (1976) and *Scum* (1977), management became anxious about the play's content – including 'the appearance on screen of a preserved penis in a specimen jar', 'a few lines pertaining to menstruation', and 'the nature of the climactic disappearance', which would have featured a naked female actor.

[120] McEwan, Ian, 'Ian McEwan Writes about His Television Plays', *London Review of Books*, vol. 3 no. 2, pp19-20.

[121] **Toby Hadoke's Who's Round** #165.

Joyce, inexperienced in making studio-based television drama, persevered and, judging by the results and the reactions from viewers and those within the BBC, made a creditable drama. It's dominated by two effective performances from Stephen Moore and Morag Hood as Simon and Mary Hulse, whose stable marriage and family life is plunged into chaos when Simon develops paranoid schizophrenia. It does borrow some elements from *The Day the Call Came*, essentially Simon's delusions about phone bugging, secret signals from cars parked in the street, and the dinner party as symbolic of the pressures associated with the middle class struggle to maintain social and work place hierarchies. Beyond this, Joyce crafts an absorbing play about how a mental health problem derails Simon and Mary's life. It explores the consequences and, for Mary, the frustration, of trying to get friends and professionals to treat her husband's condition seriously.

Unsurprisingly, Joyce's tragicomedy also refers back to Beckett. In an opening dinner party sequence, Mary recalls a dream where she is standing on an enormous, empty plain where an invisible hand gradually pushes her into the ground. Her guest, Cath, tells her 'it reminds me of a play about this woman buried in a heap of rubbish. Well, that's all that happens.'[122] Cath is referencing Beckett's *Happy Days* (1961), whose middle class housewife Winnie begins the first act buried up to her waist on a desert plain and completes the second act up to her neck. Slowly swallowed by the earth, she endlessly natters on about herself and constantly reaches into a shopping bag to retrieve various objects, projecting her fears and hopes as she tries to get through one more mundane day. It's

---

[122] **Play for Today**, *Keep Smiling*, broadcast 10 January 1980.

analogous to both Mary and Simon's own Beckettian situation as Simon succumbs to his symptoms, spending his time collecting the neighbour's rubbish.

A picnic ends disastrously when Simon pulls their car off the road into a field. Joyce handles this film sequence with a flowing camera movement that follows Mary from the car, into the field and then tracks her back to the car to show Simon collapsed onto the grass. In a distinctive scene, he exchanges a glance with another car driver waiting at a crossing and Joyce, using Simon's point of view (POV), tracks into the driver's face as his eyes swirl with vivid video effects, accompanied by Dave Greenslade's atonal electronic score. The images dissolve into solarised purple abstraction before Joyce cuts back to the car driving off. The sense of Simon being overwhelmed by his paranoia is repeated in a later studio scene where he's engulfed in a purple fog. As he looks out of the bedroom window at night, the fog travels into the room and drowns him. These are good examples of Joyce working on film and video, often using subjective POV, and combining it with video effects to portray the kind of audio and visual hallucinations that are symptomatic of this form of schizophrenia. He also uses white outs, rather than fades to black, to denote brief passages of time or interludes between scenes as Simon's condition deteriorates.

Keep Smiling demonstrates Joyce was already imbuing his studio recordings with the film techniques and genre aesthetics that would distinguish *Warriors' Gate*. He recalled:

> '...when I went in to do *Keep Smiling*, which David produced, the recording finished at 10 o'clock at night and as the second hand of the clock moved up towards 10, and I was doing the

last shot, and I said cut and it was 10 o'clock David turned to me and said, "That's the most impressive studio debut of any director I've ever seen."'[123]

At the BBC's internal Television Weekly Programme Review meeting, Keith Williams, the Head of Plays, 'liked the play and thought it well directed by Paul Joyce from Birmingham.' An aspect of the play commented on was its presentation of schizophrenia, and Rose reinforced Joyce's achievement by informing Graeme MacDonald and the other department heads that this was his debut as a television director[124].

Several months later, in the BBC's Audience Research Reports, Moore and Hood were highly praised for their work and, significantly, given he was about to be contracted by Nathan-Turner for *Warriors' Gate*, Joyce's direction and the production 'received general approbation from viewers. The camera-work and special effects were thought to have been most successful in conveying a terrifying, yet believable, atmosphere.'[125]

Soon after, Rose recommended Joyce to Nathan-Turner, who wrote back confirming Joyce had been contracted, thanked Rose for his advice and the loan of a copy of *Keep Smiling*, adding that 'I very

---

[123] **Toby Hadoke's Who's Round** #165.

[124] BBC WAC file. Television Weekly Programme Review meeting, 16 January 1980. Rose had acknowledged 'there had been some complaint about the way schizophrenia had been handled but he knew that in fact Joyce had done his homework on this.'

[125] BBC WAC file R9/7/163. Audience Research Reports, 18 March 1980.

much enjoyed the play.'[126] In June, Joyce was offered a choice of two stories by Nathan-Turner and Bidmead but found Gallagher's 'The Dream Time' appealed to him because he:

> '...liked the notion of something taking place, if you like, in the cusp of the dimensions, a place where time ceased. Being an admirer of Alain Resnais, the French film-maker, many of whose films deal with time, I thought that this would be very interesting territory to get into.'[127]

Having declared his interest in 'The Dream Time', he visited Jonathan Miller at BBC Television Centre just prior to the 18 to 24 June studio recording of Miller's production of *The Taming of the Shrew* for **The BBC Television Shakespeare** (1978-85)[128]. Joyce observed Miller and took stills of the rehearsals during the runup to the recording. He also saw two actors there, David Kincaid (who would play Lane) and Harry Waters (cast as Waldo, later renamed as 'Royce' in the camera scripts), who he recruited for *Warriors' Gate*. Graeme Harper, assigned as Joyce's production assistant on *Warriors' Gate*, recalled:

> 'When he came back, he said, "It was very interesting, because while the actors were rehearsing, Jonathan was walking around the set with his production assistant and [assistant floor manager], and they were making all these

---

[126] BBC WAC file T65/256/1. Memo to David Rose, 22 July 1980.

[127] Newman, 'Joyce Words'.

[128] Jonathan Miller is a celebrated polymath whose work embraces medicine, neurology and philosophy, acting, writing and presenting. His many achievements include directing six of the **BBC Television Shakespeare** adaptations.

notes of where he was saying he wanted the camera set-ups to be, and working it all out for him." Paul thought that was a wonderful way of working.'[129]

Joyce's later recollection that 'I always got my assistant and used them to do the camera script' suggests a similar process occurred with *Keep Smiling*, and he was acclimatised at BBC Birmingham to working this way. Joyce certainly felt that:

'I was like Miller in that the camera script was there, he would do it on the fly, you know, eyeball it, as David Hockey would say, [...] and that's how I would work. So, I didn't learn anything about camera scripts but I learned about dealing with actors.'[130]

However, Miller tempered his stylistic approach to *The Taming of the Shrew* with his own reservations, pertinent to Joyce's situation at the time, about adapting theatre for the television studio in 1980:

'There are specific problems to do with the institution of television, and specific problems to do with the medium of television. Television is really a motor-car factory in which you are required to turn out products in fixed slots of time. If you don't you will muck up the factory. You're doing work at a more rapid rate than is compatible with the quality you

[129] Rigelsford, Adrian, *Classic Who: The Harper Classics*, p36-37.
[130] Joyce, interview with author.

think it deserves. You simply have to find a corresponding form of stylisation which is suitable for a television screen.'[131]

Joyce discovered that it was difficult to fully achieve this in the BBC studio and Harper advised him that **Doctor Who** simply didn't have the luxury of five weeks' rehearsal time afforded to the production of *The Taming of the Shrew*. Joyce was expected to plan and then, after 10 days' rehearsal, record the four episodes of *Warriors' Gate*. Harper raised his concerns with Nathan-Turner, feeling Joyce was likely to adhere to his own way of working and leave completion of his studio planning and camera scripts late into rehearsals.

Papers in the archives clearly show Joyce responded to Gallagher's second draft scripts in late July, with notes pertinent to specific numbered scenes for each of the episodes. At this point the production was referred to as *Warriors' Gate*, the original title having been replaced between receipt of the second drafts and Joyce's response[132].

Joyce's episode 1 notes suggested establishing the crew and the privateer, the reasons for their arrival in the void, and Biroc's concerns about the Calibans, up front. He also requested an explanation of the mass detector's function and a stronger

---

[131] Pasternak Slater, Ann, 'Directing Shakespeare', Miller interviewed for *Quarto*, September 1980 in Miller, Jonathan and Ian Greaves, ed, *One Thing and Another: Selected Writings 1954–2016*, pp131-32.
[132] Bidmead originally suggested 'Gateway' as a title. Gallagher thought this would be too easily confused with Frederick Pohl's 1977 novel of the same name, and came up with *Warriors' Gate*.

motivation for the Doctor to remain in the void other than seeking help from the privateer to repair K-9. He recommended a more considered introduction to Biroc's arrival at the banqueting hall and asked why the silver globes – the temporal distortion bombs – never reappear later in the story[133]. For the second episode, Joyce wanted clarity about the Shogun-Caliban conflicts and why the Calibans passed through the mirrors easily. With regard to K-9, he asked Gallagher to emphasise how upsetting it was 'that he is malfunctioning.' He suggested having Aldo and Waldo hide under the table during the crew's lunch. The conversations between Adric and Romana should further underline her imminent recall to Gallifrey, and, precipitating the removal of several of Gallagher's minor characters from the rehearsal scripts, he asked 'Are Jos (and Dulles later on) necessary characters?'[134]

On episode 3, Joyce raised concerns about the 'frequently confusing' exits and entrances on the privateer He thought the Versailles garden beyond the mirror was an unconvincing indication that 'the gateway leads "anywhere".' He suggested that Biroc returned to the gateway 'to rejuvenate himself in preparation for the task ahead'[135] and alluded to H Rider Haggard's *She: A History of Adventure* (1887). This novel featured the goddess Ayesha similarly renewing herself in the flames of the Pillar of Life but also resonated with themes of decay and entropy. Some readings of *She* have articulated 19th-

---

[133] Gallagher reasoned that the bombs only functioned as a clue to the kind of forces operating at the gateway.

[134] Hull Archives, UDGA *Warriors' Gate* (file 1). Paul Joyce's notes on the second drafts of episodes 1-4, 25 July 1980.

[135] Hull Archives. Joyce's notes on the second drafts.

century fin-de-siècle anxieties about 'the relationship between savagery and civilisation via a nuanced critique of degeneration' where 'the presence of fallen empires is used as a gloss for contemporary concerns about British Empire-building.'[136] This sense of reconciling with the crises of the past in order to make sense of a postcolonial future runs through *Warriors' Gate*, both in Gallagher's script and aesthetically in its sets and costumes.

Appropriately, Joyce proposed a glimpse 'of the Shogun / Caliban fight in the distant past' to contextualise their history. Previous concerns about the confusing entrances and exits on the ship, the sudden, inexplicable reappearances of Biroc, and questions about Adric and K-9's functions to the story were included in his notes for episode 4. He also thought that the Doctor's inventive actions arrived too late into the story and, although the Doctor's final realisation about Biroc's precognition of events was 'excellent and exciting', he worried that Gallagher was not providing enough tension. The departure of Romana was 'very down-beat and blank' and he asked, 'Is this really how we want them to part?'[137]

Joyce, like Bidmead, was focused on making the structure and themes of the story more dramatically coherent. Gallagher was 'a wonderful writer and I think he came up with a terrific treatment and concept. We were trying to construct a sensible storyline where the treatment was very helpful.'[138] Gallagher, working out his notice at Granada, could not attend further script meetings and, for the

---

[136] Smith, Andrew, 'Degeneration' in Hughes, William, Punter, David and Smith, eds, *The Encyclopedia of the Gothic*, pp174-176.
[137] Hull Archives. Joyce's notes on the second drafts.
[138] Joyce, 'The Dreaming' documentary.

third drafts, dictated changes to scenes and dialogue over the phone to Bidmead. After all three attended a working lunch on 5 August 1980, Bidmead wrote to Gallagher, enclosing the rehearsal scripts for the first three episodes. In his letter he felt Gallagher was 'with us in spirit, though, when the time came to roll up our sleeves and confront the problems of the final draft.'[139] Referring to his and Joyce's restructuring of the scripts, he explained further:

> 'Our main difficulty was that although the atmosphere of your scripts was haunting and powerfully delineated, the scenes as they stood were not dramatically strong enough to sustain a hundred minutes of television. Paul Joyce [...] has been very helpful in suggesting ways to best do justice to your original concept and characters.'

Anticipating Gallagher's dissatisfaction with the way his work had been adapted, Bidmead urged:

> 'I understand perfectly from my own experience the mixed feelings with which a writer confronts "improvements" of this order; but I hope you'll share with us something of our satisfaction in a co-operative effort well done, and look forward with us to what we believe will be the high spot of this season.'[140]

It can be seen, even without all of the drafts available to compare, that Bidmead and Joyce undertook a substantial amount of work on the rehearsal scripts to modify Gallagher's original treatment and

---

[139] Hull Archives, UDGA *Warriors' Gate* (file 1). Letter to Gallagher, 7 August 1980.
[140] Hull Archives. Letter to Gallagher, 7 August 1980.

the structure, dialogue and characters from his first, second and third draft scripts. A summary of that work follows.

Episode 1

Bidmead and Joyce's rehearsal script mainly adheres to Gallagher's first draft but introduces several changes. Gallagher opens with the Doctor, Romana, Adric and K-9 in the TARDIS. They discuss her return to Gallifrey and exchange views about the random flow of the universe and the *I Ching*. This inspires Adric to toss a coin to aid their navigation through E-Space. Gallagher concludes with Biroc's hijack of the TARDIS, before bringing the privateer and its crew into the story. Lost from the rehearsal script are Gallagher's pursuit of the privateer by the Antonine Killer, already replaced in the third draft with Lane's spacewalk inspection of the damage sustained during the ship's warp jump[141].

The rehearsal script starts with the track through the privateer's interior and establishes the crew and Biroc on the bridge. Several pared-down TARDIS scenes are intercut with this. Romana's effusive dismissal of the Doctor's theory of random sampling is truncated to 'Coffee table Jung!'[142]. Adric's coin toss is matched with Aldo and Waldo's bet on Biroc's survival when Rorvik threatens him with a high-tension cable. Bidmead and Joyce's scene with Aldo and Waldo, culminating with the coin frozen in mid-air as the privateer hits a time rift, replaces Gallagher's scene where Aldo and Waldo disrupt the suspense by insisting on emptying the rubbish bins. Biroc's

---

[141] Hull Archives, UDGA *Warriors' Gate* (file 1). Gallagher's undated notes for the third draft of episode 1.
[142] *Warriors' Gate*, rehearsal script dated 10 August 1980, p18.

visualisation of the TARDIS and his escape from the privateer are not in Gallagher's draft. However, Gallagher's dialogue for Biroc's scene in the TARDIS is partially retained in the rehearsal script, although his plea to the Doctor from Gallagher's third draft ('In the name of all that's just, do not let cruelty go unchecked') is dropped along with his offer to help them escape E-Space[143].

In Gallagher's first draft, the Doctor visits the privateer after meeting Rorvik outside the TARDIS. Realising their purpose when he finds Biroc's shackles at the navigator's position, he briefly returns to the TARDIS before he joins Rorvik's search for Biroc. Bidmead and Joyce have the Doctor leave the TARDIS and immediately follow Biroc to the gateway. He doesn't meet Rorvik or visit the privateer. In the rehearsal script for episode 2, Romana encounters Rorvik outside the TARDIS. She is given Gallagher's dialogue, originally written for the Doctor. Her visit to the privateer then ends with her capture. The rehearsal script retains Gallagher's original cliffhanger, where a Gundan (renamed from Shogun) robot threatens the Doctor.

Episode 2

After the Doctor, Rorvik and Lane encounter the Shogun robot in the banqueting hall, Gallagher has the Doctor theorise about the silver time bombs and the gateway. Bidmead and Joyce transfer this to a scene where the Doctor repairs the Gundan, cutting the material about the time bombs, and it recounts the history of the slavers and the Tharks just as Rorvik and his men enter the hall.

Gallagher's scene featuring Rorvik's crew lunching in the banqueting hall is revised and incorporated later into episode 3 by Bidmead and

---

[143] Morris, 'The Fact of Fiction'.

Joyce. His scene featuring Aldo and Waldo discussing the purpose of their rubbish collections with Lane is not in the rehearsal script. After she and Adric see the damage from the Antonine missile, Gallagher has Romana first meet Laszlo when they are both imprisoned in the hold. His notes for the episode's third draft also have her theorising the privateer's motors are 'too powerful – white dwarf?'[144] but she works out that the ship is made of dwarf star alloy later in Bidmead and Joyce's episode 3. Lazlo (spelled Laszlo in Gallagher's drafts), badly burnt after Aldo and Waldo's failure to revive him, first encounters Romana in Bidmead and Joyce's episode 2 cliffhanger. This replaces Gallagher's cliffhanger, where the Doctor stumbles through the mirror to avoid gunfire from Rorvik and his men.

Episode 3

Bidmead and Joyce have the Doctor instead stumble over K-9, fall through the mirror, and meet Biroc, who explains how the mirror's healing properties could restore K-9. Gallagher has the Doctor menaced by a restored Shogun and only briefly meeting Biroc in the gardens before Romana and Laszlo arrive. She and the Doctor conclude that the gateway is the CVE leading back to N-Space and Gallifrey. Presumably based on Joyce's request to expand on Caliban history, Gallagher's third draft first establishes the Gundan's narrative eventually related to the Doctor in the rehearsal script of episode 2, and suggests the time shift that closes episode 3:

> '...he catches up with the restored Shogun robot and learns they were built by the Caliban's human slaves. He orders it to

---

[144] Hull Archives. Gallagher's undated notes for the third draft of episode 2.

finish its story and the banqueting hall appears around them with the Caliban feast – it's all "blurred, slowed down, an imperfect playback" and the Shogun burst in.'

The Doctor then castigates Biroc for reliving the past triumphs of his race. In response, he simply advises the Doctor to wait and allow events to run their course.

Bidmead and Joyce develop this with the Doctor and Biroc's conversation during the opulent feast at the restored banqueting hall. In Gallagher's draft, Laszlo provides further exposition about the gateway, suggesting Romana should trust in intuition rather than technical solutions.

Bidmead and Joyce place the feast that is interrupted by the Gundans in parallel to the modest sandwich buffet enjoyed by Rorvik's crew in the ruined banqueting hall. These scenes again fulfil Joyce's desire to play back Caliban/Thark history, strikingly achieved by cutting between the two time periods in the hall, punctuated by the Doctor knocking over the goblet of wine and the Gundan's axe splitting the table. In addition, Bidmead and Joyce layer in the threat that the void is contracting, its collapse connected to the mass anomaly created by the privateer's dwarf star alloy composition and its massive engines. This refers to Gallagher's earlier introduction of the alloy and the contraction of the void in his revised third draft of episode 1.

Gallagher's first draft of episode 3 is again structurally different from the rehearsal script. The original cliffhanger, with Adric losing his coin and marooning himself and K-9 in the void, is somewhat weaker than the rehearsal script's development of the time shift that throws the Doctor back into Rorvik's clutches. His third draft features another much different cliffhanger, where the restored Shogun encountered by the Doctor attacks Biroc as he watches Rorvik's crew through the mirror. Plunging through the mirror, the robot corrodes and Biroc escapes its clutches[145]. Gallagher also has Rorvik order his men to dig through the banqueting hall's wall to get through the mirror, only to discover 'the mirror continues seamlessly behind the wall.'[146] Rorvik's failure to bypass the mirror leaves him with the back-blast as his only option. Bidmead and Joyce change this by introducing the MZ and, in episode 4, Rorvik defaults to the back-blast when the MZ fails to blast through the mirror. Adric's seizure of the MZ also facilitates the Doctor's escape from the hall.

Episode 4

Gallagher's script has the Doctor, Romana and Laszlo returning to the TARDIS after finding the hall empty and the privateer already building up to the back-blast. Gallagher focuses on Laszlo's concern for the other slaves in the hold. When Adric suggests the Doctor and Laszlo use the damaged power couplings to shut down the ship's engines, they leave Adric, Romana and K-9 in the TARDIS. On the privateer, as the Caliban slaves are revived, the Doctor realises that Biroc has foreseen how these events would unfold. Romana takes the TARDIS forward in time to avoid the back-blast. The Doctor and Laszlo return to it on the time winds and witness the freed slaves leaving the wrecked privateer and disappearing through the mirrors. Rorvik's ghostly crew are beckoned into the gateway by a Shogun robot.

---

[145] Morris, 'The Fact of Fiction'.
[146] Hull Archives. Gallagher, 'The Dream Time', episode 3, p25.

As a way of strengthening her moral imperative and underlining the story's themes prior to her departure, Bidmead and Joyce have Romana argue they can't leave because of the slaves in the hold, and that the back-blast will accelerate the collapse of space and time. Adric proposes that this could flip them back into N-Space. Both Adric and Romana alert the Doctor to the damaged couplings in the hold indicated by Lane's clipboard. In Gallagher's episode 3, Adric noticed the clipboard but this is assigned to Romana in the rehearsal script when the Doctor and she attempt to shut the engines down.

Bidmead and Joyce's changes and additions include Aldo, Waldo and Sagan's failure to revive a slave suitable to use as the ship's navigator and Rorvik's investigation of the resulting power losses to precipitate his confrontation with the Doctor and Romana in the hold. There Biroc advises the Doctor to do nothing while Lazlo electrocutes Sagan and revives the rest of the Tharks. The rehearsal script does not resolve Romana and K-9's farewell. K-9 is carried back to the TARDIS before Romana and the Doctor attempt to stop the back-blast. On Biroc's advice they return to the TARDIS, escape the back-blast, and watch the slaves emerge from the razed privateer. The TARDIS materialises above the gardens and then heads off into N-Space. The rewritten episode 4 camera script does include their departure to assist the Tharils as seen onscreen.

Gallagher's first draft does include Romana's departure with K-9, fulfilling Bidmead's brief to write them out of the series. In the TARDIS she and the Doctor contemplate K-9's fate and her refusal to return to Gallifrey. She instead opts to remain in E-Space by learning to use the gateway as her TARDIS. The Doctor gives her K-9, knowing that by crossing through the mirrors he will be restored to full working order. Gallagher's final scene shows her with K-9 alone in the void, flipping Adric's gold star badge to decide the direction to the mirrors.

Perhaps Bidmead and Joyce were still hopeful Ward would change her mind about her decision to leave, one she and Nathan-Turner had mutually agreed in January 1980. She and Tom Baker were in the throes of a turbulent relationship and both were unhappy that her time on the series was nearly over. On 13 August, after delivering the rehearsal scripts, Nathan-Turner endorsed Joyce's contribution to them internally within the BBC and secured a one-off payment for 'extensive re-writes on scripts due to unavailability of writer' because he had 'intimate knowledge of story with immediate availability to execute urgent rewrites.'[147] Joyce did not take a credit for his contribution, originally because he wanted to avoid upsetting Gallagher, but he claimed recently that 'I delivered on time a show which was quite unusual in many, many respects. I rewrote them, which they acknowledged, paid me for but refused to give me credit.'[148] He has also observed that 'God knows what it would have ended up like if somebody else had done it, who didn't know how to write'[149].

Gallagher suggests that the reason Joyce may have been denied a credit was because crediting rewrites carried out by a director and a script editor 'wouldn't have had a hope in hell of passing Writers' Guild arbitration.'[150] This was not an unusual situation at the BBC

---

[147] BBC WAC file T65/256/1. Staff Contribution to Programmes document.
[148] **Toby Hadoke's Who's Round** #165.
[149] Joyce, interview with author.
[150] Gallagher, 'Scripting *Warriors' Gate*'.

and, internally, it had strict regulations on the commissioning, contracting and writing of scripts and would have incurred the wrath of the Writers' Guild if it was evident these had been breached. There were ways of avoiding this. For example, when David Fisher's scripts for 'A Gamble in Time' were developed into *City of Death* (1979) after an eleventh-hour rewrite by script editor Douglas Adams, producer Graham Williams, and director Michael Hayes, it was credited to an in-house alias, 'David Agnew'. Similarly, Barry Letts, also aware of the Writers' Guild's concerns about a producer writing for his own show, used a pseudonym for *The Dæmons* (1971), which he co-wrote with Robert Sloman.

Refinements to the scripts continued before rehearsals and Nathan-Turner, in Bidmead's absence, offered to discuss Letts' notes with Joyce after the readthrough on 6 September. Rehearsals eventually commenced on 10 September and rewrites were necessitated after Baker and Ward expressed their unhappiness with the scripts. Bidmead and Joyce's discussions with Barry Letts on 17 September had also resolved Letts' concerns about the way the mirrors worked for the Tharks and for Romana while proving to be a dead end for Rorvik[151]. Although Bidmead and Joyce had rewritten the scenes

---

[151] The Doctor realises this in his conversation with Biroc in episode 3. However, his line about the gateway being 'the jumping-off point for E-Space but for non-time-sensitives...' barely explains that time-sensitives and Time Lords are telepathic to an extent and able to use the mirrors whereas humans are unable to. For machines like the Gundans and K-9, it's a one-way journey. They are repaired or healed by passing through the mirror but they cannot return and remain intact.

featuring Romana and K-9's departure, an unhappy Ward complained to Nathan-Turner and Bidmead about their lack of drama. Bidmead declared that this was not a scene out of a soap opera and 'Romana's departure would be neither dramatic nor emotional.'[152] As Joyce recalled:

> 'In fact, neither Chris Bidmead, nor Steve Gallagher, nor I really confronted that part of the story, but I remember that I just had to because I'd got to the end of that page. I vaguely recall the line where the Doctor says: "Well, what a moment to choose." I thought that that was kind of enigmatic, that it summed everything up. The circumstances of the drama at that point meant that it was, literally, the moment to choose.'[153]

Several TARDIS scenes were rewritten and lines of dialogue were changed or dropped where, for example, crew member Nestor's lines were bequeathed to Packard. In episode 4's rehearsal script, before the Doctor departs with Romana to shut down the privateer's engines, the Doctor puts his hat on Adric's head and informs him he is in charge of the TARDIS if they fail to return. This was probably the remnant of several scenes where Adric was supposed to 'spend half an episode wearing the Doctor's hat and scarf' that Baker vetoed during rehearsals when he 'saw Waterhouse trying on his costume elements.'[154] This and other changes were incorporated into the camera scripts prior to production and during recording.

---

[152] *Doctor Who: The Complete History*, Volume 33, p61.
[153] Newman, 'Joyce Words'.
[154] *Doctor Who: The Complete History*, Volume 33, pp62-63.

Gallagher attended the readthrough on 6 September and visited the studio recording on 2 October. He was unhappy about the way his scripts had been treated, and later expressed this to Nathan-Turner when there was keen interest in his outline for *Terminus* (1983). He complained, after submitting his three drafts and dictating many changes over the phone late at night, that 'only 50% of my story material made it through, and none of that came from either of the rewrites. The proportion of my original dialogue was somewhere less than 10%.'[155]

It was a legitimate view. However, he admitted that, 'I'm not used to handling team input on a story. A time-served television writer would probably have sat down with Chris and Paul for a three-handed rewrite and been quite happy about doing it, but I simply don't work that way.' Given the impending rehearsal and studio dates, he saw no alternative to letting Bidmead and Joyce rewrite *Warriors' Gate*, but he 'never expected it to differ so drastically from the original.'[156] He also raised concerns that his publisher at Sphere hadn't been able to follow the story and, if he hadn't already signed a contract and been paid for his novel *Chimera*, suggested this could have affected its publication. In 1994, in his response to Joyce's interview in *In-Vision*, he provided some examples of the revisions he was unhappy with and questioned:

> 'Is this "co-authorship"? A screen composer would recognise it as something akin to "Mickey-Mousing", following the

---

[155] Hull Archives, UDGA *Warriors' Gate* (file 1). Letter to Nathan-Turner, 10 April 1981.
[156] Hull Archives, letter to Nathan-Turner.

action of an original, paraphrasing it, occasionally touching base and quoting it, some of the time going off altogether but always having to return before the structure starts to go.'[157]

Another change he referred to was the replacement of the silver temporal distortion bombs 'by a manacle of dwarf star alloy which, despite its legendary density, the Doctor is able to tote around in his coat pocket. This is what was referred to at the time as "adding in the science". It's no secret now that I wasn't impressed by what I saw.'[158] As previously noted, he contested the claim that it was Joyce's idea to use black-and-white photographs for the gardens and palace in episode 3.

However, Gallagher recently conceded this response was 'probably more contentious than it should have been and I regret that now, because life is too short for that kind of thing and, at the end of the day, we're all collaborators on the show.'[159] Likewise, Bidmead believed that, despite the disputed authorship of the scripts, a genuine collaboration had resulted, where 'Steve Gallagher's imagery, and his characters and his concept of what a story could be, was absolutely supreme. I take some credit for the script but the credit really belongs to, I think, all three of us.'[160]

In May 1980, WH Allen, the publisher of the Target Books novelisations, contracted Gallagher to adapt the serial after seeing the first draft scripts. Issues with the Writers' Guild delayed a

---

[157] Gallagher, 'Scripting *Warriors' Gate*'.
[158] Gallagher, 'Scripting *Warriors' Gate*'.
[159] **Toby Hadoke's Who's Round** #166.
[160] Bidmead, 'The Dreaming' documentary.

contract from being issued until September 1981. It was published under the pseudonym of 'John Lydecker'[161] as he wanted to separate it from subsequent novels by Stephen Gallagher and also felt uneasy taking the full credit for what he thought was 'really a team effort'. On reflection, he considered that:

> '...writing a TV script makes you an important contributor to the final product; I don't consider myself its "author" simply because I don't have total authority. As far as TV credits are concerned the fact is generally understood, but when scripts are then turned into book form the lines start blurring.'[162]

For the novelisation, he restored most of his first draft material that had fallen by the wayside during Bidmead and Joyce's rewrite. Although publisher W H Allen was delighted with the extended word count, Gallagher then encountered problems when his agent informed him 'John Nathan-bloody-Turner refused to pass the manuscript of *Warriors' Gate* because "it doesn't follow the changes made during production" and so [...] would not be a novelisation!' A drastically edited version was eventually published in 1982 that conformed to the story structure and dialogue of the televised version[163].

Such was the severe nature of his last-minute editing of the manuscript, for many years Gallagher was daunted by the prospect of reassembling the original draft. However, when BBC Audio

---

[161] Taken from the character in *An Alternative to Suicide*.

[162] Freeman, 'The Man in the Control Seat'.

[163] Hull Archives, UDGA *General Correspondence* (file 2). Letter from Film Link literary agency, 26 October 1981.

approached him in 2018 to present his original version of the novelisation as an audiobook, he found the archived material 'turned out to be a lot more complete and coherent than I'd expected. It was a massive juggle but everything fell into place.'[164]

Overall, the version released in April 2019 adheres closely to Gallagher's first draft structure, restoring the humour, dialogue, characters and the missing scenes featuring the crew and Aldo and Waldo. He makes some slight changes to the opening of episode 4 and has Biroc, rather than K-9, suggest to Adric, having lost his coin and his way through the void, that any form of sampling, rather than just a coin, will help him navigate through it. Very little of the rehearsal script structure remains, save for Biroc's escape from the privateer and a variation on the ending of episode 4 in which Romana and K-9 depart with Lazlo, rather than Biroc, through the gardens of the Tharil palace.

It would take an entire book to compare all the existing material and debate the changes to the scripts and novelisation of *Warriors' Gate* but it's clear, as Gallagher himself has said about their development, that:

> 'If you compare the broadcast script with the novelisation or with the typescripts that came out of my typewriter [...] you can more or less trace from one to the other the immense editing job that needed to be done on my material. And I freely admit that now, that it had to be cut down, and cut down, and cut down and reshaped and stuff dropped. But I

---

164 Gallagher, email to author, 11 May 2018.

will say again, you go back to that original proposal and it's all there.'[165]

Asked if he accepted there were three authors contributing to the script of *Warriors' Gate*, Joyce recently offered:

> 'I think that's right, I think it's a question of what percentage [...] Bidmead wouldn't take a third, you know, you'd have to decide whether Gallagher or I have got the greater share, but I put Bidmead down at 20%. Then you've got to decide on the 80%? Has it got Gallagher's signature on it or has it got mine? Look at the lines [...] when my sons are looking at it they're laughing at my lines. And the humour, you know, "String in the leg's gone," it's all me. If you say, ultimately, one shares the credit split with Bidmead, then you end up with "who directed it?"'[166]

---

[165] **Toby Hadoke's Who's Round** #166.
[166] Joyce, interview with author.

CHAPTER 4: FADE TO GREY

Paul Joyce's preparation of the camera scripts was, as Graeme Harper recalled, that 'he would dictate to me the shots he was going to do, and I would work it out.'[167] Harper's view was that such a lengthy process could not be accommodated within **Doctor Who**'s tight schedule. He was eventually freed of some duties to work with Joyce because, late into production, 'there was actually no other way to get it done other than follow him through the run-through of the story and make notes.'[168] Harper spent several late nights writing the camera scripts. Together with assistant floor manager Val McCrimmon and director's assistant Joyce Stansfeld, he revised them after the technical run, both to anticipate Joyce's requirements and to incorporate changes made during the day. This process was repeated during the second block of rehearsals and recordings. Later accounts from Harper, the actors, costume and effects crews praised Joyce's commitment to the production. However, in planning the show, McCrimmon considered Joyce 'an absolute con man. He couldn't actually do it so it ended up with Graeme Harper and I more or less having to do the show for him.'[169]

Although Joyce had developed the scripts, assembled a good cast, and was supported by the design and visual effects departments, his ambitions for *Warriors' Gate* were frustrated by unforeseen BBC studio management issues and the strictly monitored studio time

---

[167] Spilsbury, Tom, 'The Guv'nor', interview with Graeme Harper, DWM #380.
[168] Rigelsford, *Classic Who: The Harper Classics*, p37.
[169] Marson, Richard, *JN-T: The Life and Scandalous Times of John Nathan-Turner*, p110.

and union regulations related to overruns. These afforded him few opportunities to extemporise beyond the shot requirements in the camera scripts. Even so, Joyce had the resources available to him. Beyond the allocation of pedestal studio cameras, he specifically requested the use of lightweight camera rigs to shoot the multi-level bridge set, the handheld Ikegami camera for close-ups, inserts and POV shots, and a raft of video effects techniques including inlay, colour separation overlay (CSO) and Quantel video editing technology. As a budget-saving alternative to location filming, which he had dropped in favour of an extra studio day, Joyce took black-and-white photographs of the gardens and the interiors at Powis Castle, the medieval fortress, mansion and gardens near Welshpool. To realise the Doctor's journey through the Tharils' palace and gardens, he requested the hire of Scene Sync equipment to combine the photographs with live action recorded in the studio[170]. Nathan-Turner reluctantly fulfilled this request, having already trialled Scene Sync on *Meglos* (1980) and assessed that **Doctor Who** was unlikely to use it again[171].

---

[170] Scene Sync was a motion control rig used to enhance scenes involving CSO. Lining up two cameras for such a composite sequence, with one trained on the actors against a blue or green screen and one trained on the intended background (often a model shot), was laborious, and attempts to pan during these shots often resulted in actors sliding across the background or disappearing behind the model. Scene Sync linked the two cameras, enabled them to tilt and pan in unison and, within the CSO composite shot, could follow the movement of actors with minimal slippage, allowing for less static sequences.

[171] 'Production', *In-Vision* #50.

Some problems were out of Joyce's control but others, which seriously affected his working relationships with Nathan-Turner, Letts and the studio management team, were a result of the conflict between Joyce's working methods and the standard production mode of **Doctor Who** and many programmes made at the BBC. A strike delayed construction on the sets for the first block and recording had to be rescheduled to a week later in a different studio. This held up and trucated rehearsals for the second block when its studio recording resumed as originally scheduled. Joyce was under pressure to overlap recording of block one with rehearsals for block two.

For the ambitious opening sequence moving through the privateer's hold and up to the bridge, Joyce mixed the outputs of his pedestal cameras with shots from a handheld Ikegami camera. The Ikegami gave Joyce more freedom to travel through and pan around the set. During the recording on 24 September, studio lighting director John Dixon spotted that Joyce was incorporating the gallery steps and the studio lighting grid into his handheld shots and immediately halted the recording. In Dixon's opinion, shooting off the set was unacceptable and recording ground to a halt for two hours to dispute Joyce's incorporation of the studio infrastructure into Graeme Story's set design. Story's ultilitarian privateer set repurposed sections of the Vogon ship interior built for **The Hitchhiker's Guide to the Galaxy** (1980)[172], and Joyce considered the

---

[172] Davies, Kevin Jon, **The Hitchhiker's Guide to the Galaxy** DVD production text, episode 1, and tweet to author, 19 October 2018. The Vogon ship's corridors in the pilot episode and the B Ark's

studio lighting grid and the gallery steps were eminently suitable basic elements for inclusion in his shots of the ship. Visual effects supervisor Mat Irvine recalled that the lighting grid was 'girder work. The interior of the privateer was girder work. It didn't matter.'[173] After the first of many such instances, Joyce became exasperated:

> 'I mean everybody was against me. [...] Why are we spending time on this? [...] Because it's an important moment, it's the poetic Jean Cocteau moment, this is where your hand goes through a mirror. Do you understand? No. You're dealing with idiots. These people are not literate. They're not versed in even the mediums they're supposed to be dealing in.'[174]

Although concerned by the resulting delays, Nathan-Turner decided not to replace Joyce and stipulated he should continue under close supervision to speed up the rehearsals and recording. However, on 25 September recording was delayed again, by a health and safety dispute when several loose bolts were discovered in the scaffolding for the multi-level privateer set[175]. Joyce oversaw various shots, using Quantel video effects to distort the images in real time as the ship hit the time rift, but was unable to complete all of the TARDIS scenes. Inevitably, the production fell further behind and incurred an expensive overrun to complete the first block. This increasingly

---

corridors in episode 6 were constructed from metal fork-lift truck pallets previously used in the sets of Ridley Scott's *Alien* (1979).

[173] Irvine, Mat, 'The Dreaming'.

[174] **Toby Hadoke's Who's Round** #165.

[175] BBC WAC file T65/256/1. Closed Circuit VT Recordings: Late starts and overruns: Week 39: Production 2. Report at the end of Day 3 in the studio, 26 September 1980.

tense studio environment generated an unsparing operational report from Dixon on 29 September about the delays to recording, one that criticised Joyce for being self-indulgent and incompetent and failing to understand the working methods for making television in the BBC's studios[176].

It is difficult to get the exact measure of the contradictory accounts about the recording of *Warriors' Gate*, especially through the fog of memory. Although Joyce describes several attempts to sack him[177], the regularity of these disputes suggest that a formal dismissal was never actually enforced and Nathan-Turner, after trying to continue without him, 'reinstated' Joyce because he could best interpret the camera scripts. Joyce, Nathan-Turner and Harper spent their breaks rewriting the camera scripts to simplify and speed up the recording. As Harper acknowledged of Joyce:

> '...he was a superb director, there's no two ways about it, both with actors, and with what he wanted to get out of the text. He knew what he was doing – but gosh it was early days for him as a director! He had no sense of pace for himself, so we were very, very slow.'[178]

Dixon's report suggested this was because Joyce was applying film techniques to a multi-camera studio recording. Not only did he eyeball various unplanned shots but he also recorded a mixture of pedestal master shots and handheld camera inserts, so that he had

---

[176] Seen on screen in 'The Dreaming', Dixon's operational report was quoted in a memo from studio manager John Carter to, among others, Graeme MacDonald.
[177] Joyce, interview with author.
[178] Spilsbury, 'The Guv'nor'.

a choice of material to edit from in post-production. In effect, he was recording scenes twice. While this was standard film making technique, giving the director more choices during the editing process, it required support, time and resources to incorporate it into a taped multi-camera studio drama guided specifically by the director and vision mixer working to the camera scripts from the studio's gallery control room.

As with many dramas, *Warriors' Gate* was recorded out of order to maximise use of studio time and sets. Scenes were reassembled and episodes completed in post-production. Joyce certainly appreciated that 'you need all the time you can get afterwards in post-production'[179] and, by gathering so much coverage on his studio days, he appeared to be working toward that goal, albeit by slightly different, much slower means.

Joyce's description of *Keep Smiling* as 'more of an original television piece'[180] suggests that his atypical approach to *Warriors' Gate* was influenced by Rose's view that the differences between television and film were becoming less rigid. Although he saw an opportunity to experiment and apply film techniques, both editorially and aesthetically, to the production, he was cautious and believed 'you don't say, "I'm trying to contort the system and make it into a film studio" [...] You just incrementally try and do it.'[181] Technically ambitious and time-consuming, this approach eventually led to a very tired Joyce realising he needed to delegate to Harper during the second block of recording. The question of authorship re-emerges at

---

[179] **Toby Hadoke's Who's Round** #165.
[180] Joyce, interview with author.
[181] Joyce, 'The Dreaming'.

this point, with indications that both Harper and Nathan-Turner stepped in to direct in Joyce's absence. Harper kept the production running, setting up and directing scenes under Joyce's supervision during the second block and, with Joyce present in the control room, he and Nathan-Turner ran the studio floor on the final day of recording[182]. Joyce recalled:

> 'There was never any question that I wouldn't either turn up for, or complete, any stage of the production and the only delays to studio sessions would have been caused by the dispute. It's also quite untrue that "My state of health would not carry me through the day." I think that's either the residue of what they were going to say had they taken me off it, or that somebody must have looked at me and thought, "That man looks unwell." Well, to be honest, I probably did look unwell. I was without doubt depressed by the way a potentially terrific show was somehow slipping from my grasp, by all these people saying "You can't do this; you can't do that."'[183]

The redress of the banqueting hall set between 2 and 3 October demanded that Joyce complete the scenes of the feast in the 'new' banqueting hall before its overnight transformation into the cobwebbed 'old' hall. Faced with the prospect of shooting several actors around the banqueting table with five cameras, Joyce was concerned about achieving the correct left to right and right to left

---

[182] *Doctor Who: The Complete History*, Volume 33, p66-67.
[183] Newman, 'Joyce Words'.

eye lines. To avoid crossing eye lines, Harper helped with the camera placements and directed some of these scenes. Joyce admitted:

> 'I lost the plot of what we were supposed to be looking at. I know now what you do. If I shoot, as I have done, some classical music [...] you shoot everything you can and then you stitch it together afterwards. And you don't cross lines then because you've got multiple choices. That's what I should have done.'[184]

On 4 October, Harper and Nathan-Turner helped Joyce complete several sequences in the void, at the entrance to the privateer and in the passageway behind the mirror. Although he acknowledged Joyce had to delegate to him, Harper rejects the assertion he directed a significant amount of *Warriors' Gate*:

> 'You see this is where I have a problem. That was all a long time ago, and I don't want to blacken the man's name. I think he's been insulted, and I never meant to insult him, because it was still absolutely his direction. Now, I wasn't a director then, although I had aspirations. So when I wrote the camera script, I'm sure he probably changed some of it. But having done that, a) I was knackered because I'd been staying up all night writing the camera scripts, and b) I had to run two massive studio days of quite complex stuff, so I was very tired. We had some quite serious problems in the studio.'[185]

Joyce found the post-production process equally disheartening and rewarding. His working relationship with composer Peter Howell was

---

[184] **Toby Hadoke's Who's Round** #165.
[185] Spilsbury, 'The Guv'nor'.

productive, but October's gallery-only session to complete the electronic video effects, and the editing sessions overseen by Nathan-Turner, were difficult. Working with electronic effects operator Robin Lobb on slowing down and freezing the spinning coin in mid-air as the privateer hits the time rift, Joyce's determination to push technology to the limit provoked further discussion. A larger, more detailed, 60mm version of the 100 Imperial coin was shot several times falling onto a piece of flat flooring. During post-production, an out-of-focus image of the bridge was inlayed into the background and the image of the coin was slowed down, frozen at its highest point and zoomed into using Quantel. For Joyce this was an important image, a signifier that time had stood still, and he 'needed that coin to be large, believable and right there, sort of in your face. And every time it was done it was too small.'[186] Joyce's demands could not be met as each attempt to zoom in produced a degraded, pixelated image. The pixelation was a result of trying to maintain the resolution of the image, but similar qualities were later used deliberately in the slow zoom into Janet Fielding's eye in *Kinda* (1982) and the effects added to the Dalek explosion in *Revelation of the Daleks* (1985). Despite these setbacks, Mat Irvine was struck by Joyce's commitment to the production and how much support he gave to the design and visual effects departments:

> 'I always felt in control over what was needed effects-wise on *Warriors' Gate*, and I think all the other designers felt the same way too. [...] undoubtedly [Joyce's] greatest skill was communication. Everybody knew what was happening all the

---

[186] Joyce, 'The Dreaming'.

time, and who was supposed to be doing what things, which for the servicing side of television is as close to an ideal as you can ever get.'[187]

While overseeing Joyce's editing of the episodes, 'Nathan-Turner had very, very strong views about what could cut (together) and couldn't and I seemed to be always having to deal with pedantic detail, questions about pedantic things where the larger picture was not being seen.'[188] For example, Nathan-Turner's correspondence with Joyce suggested a number of re-edits to part of episode 4 but with the positive caveat that 'otherwise the first half of the episode looks great.'[189] Joyce recalled:

> 'when he saw the episodes, John Nathan-Turner said: "They're terrific. I don't understand what the hell they're about, but they're great!" So, he was very generous then, and I realised that my expectations for the show had been far too ambitious. I'd just wanted to extend things a bit, for myself and the programme, from the usual.'[190]

Although he made positive comments about the finished episodes, Nathan-Turner wrote to MacDonald and admitted that his choice of Paul Joyce as director:

> '...was an error of my judgement to engage someone, who works so slowly, nevertheless imaginatively, and who has so little experience of the speed at which a **Doctor Who** needs

---

[187] Irvine, Mat, 'Cause an Effect', *In-Vision* #50.
[188] **Toby Hadoke's Who's Round** #167.
[189] BBC WAC file T65/256/1. Letter to Joyce, 26 November 1980.
[190] Newman, 'Joyce Words'.

to work (though he was highly recommended) and I take full responsibility.'[191]

At the Television Weekly Programme Review meetings in January 1981 MacDonald did not register the brouhaha about Joyce's work, the disputes with Dixon and the overruns, merely acknowledging the increased ratings with the transmission of episode 2 and the earlier scheduling of episode 3[192]. Joyce wrote to Nathan-Turner that January, thanking him for the opportunity to direct *Warriors' Gate*, and reflected:

> 'Although we undoubtedly had some "creative disagreements" I must say that your opinions were always fair and directly delivered – a refreshing and unusual characteristic these days! Thank you also for your very supportive attitude when we encountered difficulties in the studio and with post-production for reasons outside our control.
>
> 'I do hope the very encouraging viewing figures for the first episode were at least held to for parts 3 and 4[193]. I feel sure the programme has taken on a new lease of life under your producership, and that the new season will bring great credit to you for the ideas and energies you have injected into it.'[194]

---

[191] Nathan-Turner's memo to MacDonald appears on screen in 'The Dreaming'.

[192] BBC WAC file. Television Weekly Programme Review meetings, 14 and 21 January 1981.

[193] *Warriors' Gate* episode 3 hit 8.3 million on 17 January 1981, the highest figure of the season.

[194] BBC WAC file T65/256/1. Letter from Joyce, 26 January 1981.

As is often the case with the contradictory accounts of *Warriors' Gate*'s production, matters don't get any clearer because Joyce has since questioned the veracity of his letter of 26 January:

> 'Anyone reading the letter you wish to publish that I wrote him with any knowledge of the history [of *Warriors' Gate*] will wonder who is trying to fool whom. Did my turncoat agent at the time, who sided with the BBC and refused to represent me after the programmes were completed, suggest I do so? Was it pure irony, with my tongue in my cheek? Frankly I cannot remember, but the truth is that N-T had an ambition to succeed in his role as strongly as I did in mine; the difference is that I understood his limitations only too well and he really had no idea of mine. Nor of what I was trying to achieve. Ultimately of course the BBC mafia supported him, and my career there ended on the transmission of the programmes.'[195]

Joyce's correspondence with Nathan-Turner did continue in 1981, when he thanked him for sending the final viewing figures and requested a copy of *Warriors' Gate* on VHS. There may have been a pretext for this, in that he was hoping to meet with Nathan-Turner for a drink, perhaps to clear the air in the hope that further work on

---

[195] Quoted from a statement emailed to the author, 10 August 2018. Joyce was contacted about the letter by the production team working on the then forthcoming Blu-ray collection of season 18, requesting its inclusion in the PDF material on the release. Joyce asked for his prepared statement to be published with the letter in the PDF material. The current author was also asked to include the comments here in context with the quotes from the original letter.

Doctor Who would come his way. His letter of 24 March offering to drop in, pick up the tape and have a drink with Nathan-Turner did not receive a direct response. However, Nathan-Turner's secretary noted the drinks invitation on the bottom of Joyce's earlier letter and a curt response of 'I may be out!' was appended in pencil[196].

It's interesting to compare Joyce's experiences to those of director Lovett Bickford, who had been encouraged to apply his own idiosyncratic visual style and pace to **Doctor Who** earlier that year. Letts had recommended the former BBC staff director, recently turned freelance, to Nathan-Turner for *The Leisure Hive* after Bickford had directed Letts' production of **The History of Mr Polly** (1980). Unlike Joyce, Bickford began as an assistant floor manager at the BBC in 1965, working in that capacity on **Doctor Who**'s *The War Machines* (1966) and *The Moonbase* (1967), and subsequently enjoyed a career within the BBC as a production assistant and production unit manager. The inexperienced Bickford was 'a frustrated film director, who liked to have total control over the lighting and camera angle of every shot. He also believed in making dramas as fast-paced as possible.'[197] Nathan-Turner, ambitious to modernise **Doctor Who**, encouraged Bickford to experiment:

> 'John Nathan-Turner and I were striving to do something new and different. We were pushing the boundaries of a studio-based system that wasn't really geared for it, and that was difficult. I think that the first time you do something, you

---

[196] BBC WAC file T65/256/1. Noted on the letter from Joyce, 20 February 1981.

[197] 'Production', *In-Vision* #46, *The Leisure Hive*.

inevitably undergo a learning process because you've never done it before. Therefore, I had a freer hand than subsequent directors.'[198]

Bickford planned *The Leisure Hive* as a feature-length comic strip, using a handheld camera to incorporate low-angle shots, rapid cutaways and close-ups. Nathan-Turner agreed to allocate an additional studio day as time was needed to test run the new Quantel video effects console and incorporate complex CSO effects during recording[199]. Bickford's accrual of separate multiple takes and his 'preference for only using two cameras, or sometimes even just one handheld camera, for many live-action scenes had meant that a lot of shots scheduled for block one had not been completed and would have to be done in block two.'[200] *The Leisure Hive* was as much a learning curve for Nathan-Turner, who was reprimanded for allowing the overruns to incur yet another studio day for the second block, taking the production significantly over budget[201]. It may have been the reason why Bickford did not direct for the series again.

Perhaps Nathan-Turner's own inexperience as a new producer working closely with directors provides a context to the difficult relationship he had with Joyce. Bidmead believed the aim to modernise **Doctor Who** was itself challenged by the BBC's institutionalisation:

'There was this extraordinary polarity that there were people who regularly worked inside **Doctor Who** for whom it was just

---

[198] Hearn, Marcus, 'Directing Who: Lovett Bickford,' DWM #191.

[199] *Doctor Who, The Complete History*, Volume 32, p31.

[200] 'Production', *In-Vision* #46.

[201] *Doctor Who, The Complete History*, Volume 32, p42.

Doctor Who – it was the "We'll get through it, we'll get it done, there are certain minimum standards and we're already working to them so let's get this thing on" that was the prevailing atmosphere about **Doctor Who** – and then there were these guys who floated in, there were your Lovett Bickfords and your Paul Joyces who were going to make great works of art out of this thing. It was kind of wonderful to have them there but even as they were there you realised they were pissing into the wind because this was not how **Doctor Who** works.'[202]

Nathan Turner not only found his creative licence limited by budget and resources within the established practices of the BBC but he also struggled to reconcile the ambitions of certain directors with those practices. Initially, his open-door policy for directors and writers sought to rejuvenate the narratives and aesthetics of **Doctor Who** as it entered a new decade. For example, Joyce and Bickford were less experienced directors than Terence Dudley and Peter Moffat, who had both been directing television drama since the late 1950s, but they brought a progressive attitude to what they could achieve in the studio. Bickford gave *The Leisure Hive* a real sense of style and pace and Joyce's experience of theatre and film culture, writing, film directing and editing impacted significantly on bringing the non-linear narrative of *Warriors' Gate* to the screen. Peter Grimwade, a former BBC production assistant turned director, brought his dynamism to *Full Circle* (1980) and *Logopolis* and his visual flair and pace peaked in season 19's *Kinda* and *Earthshock* (1982).

---

[202] **Toby Hadoke's Who's Round** #147, 'Christopher Bidmead Part 1'.

Nathan-Turner established a mixture of trusted, experienced directors and youngbloods but there were often personality clashes with younger, less experienced directors. In early 1983, Grimwade was originally assigned to direct 'The Return', Eric Saward's script featuring the Daleks. Industrial action forced its cancellation and, while commiserating about the situation, Grimwade's relationship with Nathan-Turner deteriorated after a misunderstanding about a lunch invitation. When it was remounted later that year as *Resurrection of the Daleks* (1984), Grimwade was not invited to direct and, his ties to the series severed, he contributed only one final script (*Planet of Fire*) to the series in 1984. Those who did offer a similar dynamism, like Harper when he returned to direct *The Caves of Androzani* (1984), were gradually diluted by others who, in Joyce's view, were 'just calling shots, really.'[203] Nathan-Turner was perhaps wary of directors whose agency threatened to outshine his own. Peter Davison, recalling his own frustrations with directors, 'felt that John leant towards directors who he could push around so that there would be a lot of bullying going on about certain things, quite often to get the thing done. And maybe that was necessary. But they weren't very spirited.'[204]

Nathan-Turner and Letts both thought Joyce was more suited to film directing. Of his direction on *Warriors' Gate*, Joyce asked Nathan-Turner: 'OK John, [...] what did you think of that? He said, "Well, I think you're a filmmaker and I think you should be doing top-end

[203] Joyce, 'The Dreaming'.
[204] Davison quoted in Marson, *JN-T: The Life and Scandalous Times of John Nathan-Turner*, p174.

drama. That's clearly where you're talented."' Likewise, Joyce's own view of Nathan-Turner's abilities were that he:

> '...should have done Bill Cotton's job, as [...] controller of light entertainment on BBC One. I was right about him and he was right about me. Neither of us got the ambition that the other suggested as appropriate. That's what he would have been great at in those years. Handled Morecambe and Wise. He could have done all that.'[205]

Many fans have argued that through Nathan-Turner's casting of light entertainment stars, comedians and comic actors, from Beryl Reid in *Earthshock* and Alexei Sayle in *Revelation of the Daleks* to Ken Dodd in *Delta and the Bannermen* (1987), he was perhaps vicariously fulfilling that ambition. Through these choices, as well as his briefings to script editors about new companions and particular overseas locations the series could use, his era as producer was often regarded by colleagues and fans alike as one that was eventually determined, rightly or wrongly, by his creative organisation, budgeting and casting rather than his editorial judgement or nurturing and supporting his directors and writers. Harper's view was similar:

> 'John's real gift was variety, doing a variety show. John Nathan-Turner should have been doing that kind of show, because he was brilliant, he could do a big musical production [...] but he could also do fantastic drama and **Doctor Who** was always fantastic. I think he was kept in that position too long.

---

[205] **Toby Hadoke's Who's Round** #167.

I think he kept it alive as best he could with as little as possible, with nothing – his budgets were cut down year after year.'[206]

Nathan-Turner's tenure spanned a period of transition when, as predicted by Rose, film and television started to converge and the hierarchies between the two grew less distinct. It corresponds to his laudable determination to keep **Doctor Who** in production during a decade that saw huge changes in the television industry, and where the programme's fortunes changed as the BBC became indifferent to it and Nathan-Turner unsuccessfully attempted to move on to other projects.

---

[206] **Toby Hadoke's Who's Round** #213, 'Graeme Harper Part 1'.

CHAPTER 5: CINEMATIC AND VIDEOGRAPHIC

The use of film in television drama had increased since the 1960s and, as technology advanced, filming on location was becoming the standard, particularly when directors and producers, like David Rose or Tony Garnett, demanded a sense of place and realism in their productions. Euston Films made similar inroads by filming, rather than taping, all their crime dramas on location. This influenced other dramas in terms of aesthetics, pacing and editing. As studio taping was usurped by film in drama production, the merging of filmed television and the British film industry was achieved at Channel 4 in 1982 with its **Film on Four** (1982-98) strand, inaugurated by Rose. There, writers and directors who had worked extensively in television had access to higher budgets and the incentive 'of making films that could gain a cinema release rather than the solitary television screening that most single plays achieved.'[207]

When Joyce worked at the BBC there were established television directors, like Philip Saville, Stephen Frears and Alan Clarke, who had worked in the British film industry and would continue to do so, and theatre and opera directors, such as Richard Eyre and Elijah Moshinsky, having not previously directed or produced television, coming in to make studio-based and filmed drama at the BBC. Moshinsky cut his teeth on **The BBC Television Shakespeare** under the auspices of Jonathan Miller, who had taken over as producer in 1980. Eyre had worked as artistic director at Nottingham Playhouse before he became a producer and director on **Play for Today** in 1978. His career eventually spanned theatre, television and cinema.

---

[207] Cooke, Lez, *British Television Drama: A History*, p139.

Joyce came from a similar background, and perhaps this was the career path he desired, too. After *Warriors' Gate*, he continued to work in television and also returned to making documentary films. He rekindled his assocation with Rose when he directed *Summer Lightning* (1984), a **Film on Four** co-production with Raidió Teilifís Éireann (RTÉ), and then followed this with Barry Pilton's satire on Thatcherism, *Everyone a Winner* (1988) for the Channel 4 anthology of plays **Tickets for the Titanic** (1987-88). However, a more sustained career in television and film drama eluded him:

> 'I thought my career was on track but it didn't happen, somehow. [...] I don't know if it was because of, you know, the flak, of the fallout, the smoke clearing from the **Doctor Who**. I don't know.'[208]

If Joyce's work on *Warriors' Gate* was, essentially, that of an auteur film director, then it raises questions about what he hoped to achieve by bringing a film consciousness to **Doctor Who**. Using film language and construction to tell the story in a visually dynamic way, he sought to make his work distinct from certain directors who operated within what Bidmead called 'the prevailing atmosphere' of **Doctor Who**. Joyce's attempt to enhance **Doctor Who** as a visual text, one made primarily in the studio rather than on location, and to embrace a sense of pace, fluidity, depth and space and expand the range of shot choices open to directors, cast him as something of a Janus-like figure. He was simultaneously looking back over his shoulder, influenced by directors who had, despite certain limitations, worked creatively and imaginatively in both television and cinema, and looking forward at what he thought was about to

---

[208] **Toby Hadoke's Who's Round** #167.

happen to television drama production. According to Joyce this contradiction was not lost on his mentor David Rose: 'He said, "Joyce, I can't quite work you out. You're either a genius or a charlatan."'[209] He saw his career as a television director not only being shaped by his affinity with film culture but also by the medium's evolution, where film would replace tape and the cinematic would inform its stylistic development. Consequently, when television drew on cinema and the cinematic to validate itself as a medium it extended the debate about specific television styles and how previously the old hierarchies between television and cinema had categorised television style as inferior.

Television style and quality was often deemed aesthetically poorer, where television had used intimate, domestic scale presentation as opposed to the epic scope of cinema. However, the potential of the cinematic in television was intimated in the 1990 Broadcasting Act, which equated quality television with prestigious, filmed literary adaptations like **Brideshead Revisted** (1981) and **The Jewel in the Crown** (1984), programmes that were well-made, well-funded and accorded with the high standards of the broadcaster or producers, and reflected their branding. By 1990, studio drama either recorded on tape or a hydrid of tape and film was an anomaly in a period when multi-camera production was more or less reserved for sitcoms or soaps. **Doctor Who** was by then no longer in production and, as a multi-camera production shot entirely on video tape, it had been deemed somewhat anachronistic. As television and film merged, the single play had either been absorbed into **Film on Four** or the BBC's television film anthologies **Screen One** (1989-93) and **Screen Two**

---

[209] Joyce, interview with author.

(1985-94). The majority of drama series and plays were being shot on various film formats. Eventually, production became fully digital and, along with the increasing importance of exporting programmes to global markets, this evolved into working on high-definition digital formats that could then be processed in post to look like film.

As public broadcasters faced competition from home entertainment formats, subscription satellite, cable and streaming services, the cinematic also became the signifier of an enhanced visual style demanded by the narratively rich television drama that would emerge after the 1990s. With the ability to realise spectacular imagery, television gradually adopted the visual panache and the required concentration of big-budget cinema. John Thomas Caldwell called this 'televisuality', and referred to specific visual styles – the cinematic and the videographic – to demarcate the high-profile, long-form, quality dramas from lower-budget music television, reality shows or rolling news channels. The cinematic 'brought to television spectacle, high production values and feature-style cinematography' and the videographic, with its 'appreciation of multiple electronic feeds, image-text combinations, videographics', was mass-market, hyperactive and effects driven[210]. Caldwell noted that in America science fiction and fantasy television drama was a beneficiary of this televisuality as it acquired higher budgets and sought to meet the expectations of an audience used to cinema's high production values and sophisticated visual effects. More recently television's convergence with cinema has shifted focus back

[210] Caldwell, John Thornton, *Televisuality: Style, Crisis and Authority in American Television*, p12-13.

to story and character development, as its ability to tell long-form narratives encourages prolific film directors to re-engage with it.

However, the application of the cinematic to high budget dramas made since 1990 did not necessarily transfer to other television genres and, more importantly, it ignored the inherent stylistic qualities that already existed in much of the low and high budget television programmes made before then. As Hannah Andrews noted, the cinematic 'tends to refer to a particular range of stylistic choices: 'arty' off-kilter framing, the use of wide-angle establishing shots, glossy cinematography, the presence of high-profile stars. 'Cinematic' is a meaningless adjective, because in reality the stylistic choices available to cinema and (particularly single-camera) television in framing, lighting, mise-en-scène and so on are more or less identical.'[211] Therefore, it can be argued that television made before its convergence with cinema was as rich and original in televisual terms, and that 'the development of television drama is not a story of the steady emancipation from theatrical values towards the cinematic, but one where producers were able to choose from a range of stylistic features.'[212]

Although Caldwell applied his theories to American television, Matt Hills proposed that, despite its temporary demise prior to the developments Caldwell theorised about, **Doctor Who** was particularly appreciated by its audience for its televisuality:

---

[211] Andrews, Hannah, *Television and British Cinema: Convergence and Divergence Since 1990*, pp29-30.
[212] Jacobs, Jason, *The Intimate Screen: Early British Television Drama*, p117.

'We might suggest that **Doctor Who** was "televisual" avant la lettre and hence that televisuality was already lurking within BBC TV production at least from 1963 onwards, awaiting its ultimate US glorification. Extreme narrative and visual gambits: Dalekmania, anyone? Or Saturday night Zarbi or Zygons? Or, the beautifully blank, Cocteau-derived mise-en-scène of *Warriors' Gate*.'[213]

By Caldwell's definition, the televisuality of **Doctor Who** is perhaps less cinematic and more videographic because it was a studio drama made on tape. Yet, some directors making studio-based drama were still able to select from and embed a wide range of stylistic features within their productions. By 1980, **Doctor Who** was, to a degree, evolving in parallel with the fast-paced editing and image processing that dominated the emerging music video genre as well as the effects-driven science fiction cinema that had dominated the box office since the release of *Star Wars* (1977). To borrow Caldwell's terminology, the videographic styles and pacing of music video influenced the growing sense of hyperactivity in the series as, under certain directors, it not only became more sophisticated technically, but also married storytelling to meaningful settings, sharper editing and varying types of shots.

Joyce's work on *Warriors' Gate* also reflected the history of the experimental, film-influenced aesthetic threaded throughout the development of television drama that stretched back to the groundbreaking work of the Langham Group at the BBC in the 1950s,

---

[213] Hills, Matt, 'Televisuality without Television? The Big Finish Audios and Discourses of Tele-centric **Doctor Who'**, in Butler, David, ed, *Time and Relative Dissertations in Space*, pp284-86.

whose interest 'in the connections between the aesthetics of television and of avant-garde film' would influence the experimentation of the 1960s, filtering into television drama a combination of documentary techniques, non-naturalistic use of montage, music and visual effects[214]. Mervyn Pinfield, the associate producer of **Doctor Who** in 1963, had worked with the group 'on experimental aesthetic forms, using inlay, overlay and split screens. His experiments with video feedback generated the cloud-like streams in **Doctor Who**'s title sequence.'[215] As Hills suggests of the programme's televisuality, this confirms that, even as far back as 1963, there was an alchemy between the experimental and the conventional in how the television studio space could be used narratively and visually in **Doctor Who**. This approach coincided with the publication of Troy Kennedy Martin's essay 'Nats Go Home' in 1964, which called for a style of television drama that eschewed naturalism in favour of new forms of visual storytelling.

Doctor Who's directors managed to achieve, often by stealth, similar aims. Lovett Bickford opened *The Leisure Hive* with the often derided tracking shot across Brighton beach. It has been suggested this was either an homage to Luchino Visconti's *Death in Venice* (1971) or, as Bidmead noted, to the work of Visconti's contemporary

---

[214] Bignell, Jonathan, and Stephen Lacey, 'Introduction' in Bignell, Jonathan, and Stephen Lacey, eds, *British Television Drama: Past, Present and Future*, p6.

[215] Bignell, 'Space for "Quality": Negotiating with the Daleks' in Bignell, Jonathan and Stephen Lacey, eds, *Popular Television Drama: Critical Perspectives*, p82.

Michaelangelo Antonioni[216]. Playing on *Death in Venice*'s images and themes of decay and renewal, with the fourth Doctor's retreat to a deckchair on a windswept beach offering a sense of the entropy stalking him throughout season 18, this 'excessive new visual style seemed to imply something beyond the simple telling of a story in a straightforward manner.'[217] Earlier examples included director Ken Grieve's use of Steadicam, a camera rig then little known in the industry, which gave the location shoot for *Destiny of the Daleks* (1979) a certain cinematic fluidity, or David Maloney's strikingly surreal location filming for the nightmarish third episode of *The Deadly Assassin* (1976). It's notable that, while these were shot on film, Joyce was, by all intents and purposes, trying to apply that aesthetic to studio recordings rather than on location.

When *Warriors' Gate* went into production, studio drama aesthetics encompassed more sophisticated video editing and processing techniques and, as noted, many directors were making remarkable dramas using a distinct visual syntax to tell their narratives, beyond the conventional multi-camera manipulation of character and dialogue where studio drama equated to naturalism.

The creative use of the studio on *Warriors' Gate* was not without precedent and, as David Rolinson notes, during the transmission of *Full Circle* and *The Keeper of Traken* (1981), experimental single plays

---

[216] *The Leisure Hive*, episode 1, DVD commentary. Bidmead cites Antonioni's slow pace and painterly compositions of landscape as inspiring Bickford's sequence. Patrick Mulkern refers to Visconti and *Death in Venice* in his 2011 *Radio Times* appraisal of *The Leisure Hive*.
[217] Booy, Miles, *Love and Monsters: The Doctor Who Experience, 1979 to the Present*, p44.

directed by Philip Saville and John McGrath were shown on BBC One[218]. In 1981's *The Journal of Bridget Hitler,* made for **Playhouse** (1974-83), Saville was eschewing naturalism and deliberately exposing the artifice of television with the use of:

> 'embedded textual quotes, real historical footage and photographic sequences, strongly associated with documentary, and others, such as unusual Quantel videographic effects and CSO backdrops, more suggestive of the aesthetics of music programmes such as **Top of the Pops**, or graphic techniques used on the news.'[219]

While Saville was making *Bridget Hitler,* prolific playwright, television and theatre director John McGrath was using Quantel, CSO and the manipulation of still images 'in an exploratory way, in order to achieve some patently non-naturalistic effects' in his two-part **Play for Today**, *The Adventures of Frank* (1980)[220].

Joyce's videographic style also acknowledged the relationship between **Doctor Who** and the technical developments within the presentation of the weekly chart show **Top of the Pops** (1964-2006), which increasingly offered a shared area for televisual experimentation. Throughout the 1970s the show regularly exposed

---

[218] Rolinson, David, '(Times and) Spaces of Television – **Doctor Who**: *Warriors' Gate* (1981)'.

[219] Panos, Leah, 'Mixing Genres in the Studio: **Playhouse**: The Journal of Bridget Hitler (BBC 2, 6/2/81)'.

[220] Cooke, Lez, 'An Experiment in Television Drama: John McGrath's *The Adventures of Frank'* in Mulvey, Laura and Jamie Sexton, eds, *Experimental British Television*, p111.

the British public to the hit parade using all manner of analogue camera, mixing desk and switching tricks, including repeated zooms, fish eye and split lens techniques, electronic inlays, overlays and dissolves, solarisation and CSO. Many techniques were developed in-house by BBC technicians. For example, in the mid-1960s **Top of the Pops** 'used an engineer-designed solid-state wipe machine which could generate interesting "rolling diamond" wipes between cameras.'[221] Both shows shared a portable inlay trolley to produce inserts using ad hoc methods that generated interesting images. 'An electronic effect might be tried on **Doctor Who**, then if they got it right, it would appear in **Top of the Pops**' before it filtered out to other productions[222]. CSO was a videographic technique that made an impact as 'an alternative means of achieving a spectacular visual style' in prestigious productions such as James MacTaggart's innovative *Candide* (1973) for **Play of the Month** (1965-1983), but it had already been trialed by the BBC in **The Gnomes of Dulwich** in 1968[223] and, after carrying out some initial tests in August 1969, it was used by producer Barry Letts and director Timothy Coombe in *Doctor Who and the Silurians* (1970). A staple component of the video effects created for the original series until it ceased production

[221] Newnham, Bernard, 'Inlay, Overlay and CSO'.

[222] Wood, Tat, 'How Good Do the Special Effects Have to Be?' in *About Time: The Unauthorised Guide to Doctor Who #3 – 1970-1974: Seasons 7 to 11*, p417.

[223] Panos, Leah, 'Stylised Worlds: Colour Separation Overlay in BBC Television Plays of the 1970s' in *Critical Studies in Television*, Vol 8, No. 3 (Autumn 2013).

in 1989, it evolved into the green screen compositing technique used currently.

Electronic video techniques became more sophisticated in the 1980s and eventually incorporated the use of Quantel. The Quantel 5000 effects showing Biroc striding through the void and leaving behind him a juddering physical trail were apparently created by accident when the images were processed by Robin Lobb using the Quantel's framestore technology[224]. The 5000 was one of the first digital video effects systems and a relatively recent BBC acquisition. However, the public probably first experienced these effects with the October 1978 **Top of the Pops** airing of The Jacksons' music video for 'Blame it on the Boogie', made by effects house Image West using the Quantel 3000 and the Scanimate analog computer system. The titular brothers' dancing created electronic trail effects throughout the performance. Joyce believed the trail effects used on Biroc created the 'poetic feeling of a creature who has the ability to pass through time and space and who has special skills'[225], rather than a talented exponent of song and dance. The technique certainly sells Biroc's claim to be the 'shadow of my past and your future'[226] when he bursts into the TARDIS and confronts the Doctor and Romana, and was an example of how the purely videographic techniques of music video were influencing television production at the time.

By the autumn of 1979 Quantel was being used on **Top of the Pops** to zoom into and slide images around, split and re-arrange them on screen. Lobb was responsible for the electronic effects in *The Leisure*

---

[224] Wiggins, *Warriors' Gate* DVD production text, episode 1.
[225] Joyce, 'The Dreaming'.
[226] *Warriors' Gate*, episode 1.

Hive and in *Warriors' Gate*. He not only oversaw the Quantel effects of Biroc running out-of-phase through the void and the line of Tharils leaving the wrecked privateer but also the time ripple effects on the bridge, the glows and solarisation applied to the Tharils, the zoom into Biroc's eye and the frozen spinning coin, the mirror effects and, most importantly, the Scene Sync work, compositing colour images of the Doctor, Romana and the Tharils into the black-and-white images of Powis Castle. These were completed in collaboration with Joyce, with the last being an example of how Joyce realised the videographic technique specified for the scenes in the gardens and palace described in Gallagher's scripts, and understood its aesthetic marriage to the work of Cocteau and Resnais.

Warriors' Gate has, in hindsight, been described as looking 'like a pop video. Specifically, it looks New Romantic.'[227] As if to emphasise the point the *Warriors' Gate* DVD documentary 'The Dreaming' opens with a snippet of Visage's quintessential New Romantic ditty 'Fade to Grey', released as a single in December 1980. Even so, the video to Spandau Ballet's single 'To Cut a Long Story Short', released that November, positively oozes New Romantic cred and a *Warriors' Gate* vibe. A standard band performance video, where the lads are bedecked in a riot of tartan, flowing shirts, kilts and breeches, it opens with singer Tony Hadley fading into view in the video's mist-enshrouded, candelabra- and web-festooned London Dungeon location.

The production of *Warriors' Gate* began as the New Romantic movement was gaining media attention and when music, film and fashion were, like **Doctor Who**, about to be re-energised during a

---

[227] Miles, and Wood, *About Time #5*, p64.

time of social, economic, and political transformation in Britain. This period also saw a resurgence of underground filmmaking, the mainstreaming of electronic music and a rebirth of British fashion. Each of these pockets of creativity signalled a merging of high art and the avant-garde with a more populist manifesto and *Warriors' Gate* reflected this in how it meshed together the aesthetics of television, the music video and European cinema with British New Wave SF.

Indeed, the influence of the New Romantic style on June Hudson's costume designs could be traced to Helen Robinson and Steph Raynor of PX. In 1978, the first PX shop based in Covent Garden 'dispensed the various angular looks of early New Romantic' and by 1980, these had evolved into a 'romantic' look that 'smacked of Byron and buccaneers.' This was before Vivienne Westwood created her romantic pirate gear, eventually donned by the likes of Adam Ant and BowWowWow. The frilly shirt would become the single image 'of what it meant to be New Romantic', much to the eventual chagrin of the movement that spawned it[228]. Hudson, who had been working on **Doctor Who** since 1978, was likely aware of these emerging trends as well as ongoing developments in textile design and materials. However, her designs for the Tharils were specifically drawn from their Cocteau-inspired description in the scripts:

> 'I instantly pictured the Lion People [Tharils] as pirates, because they were described as sailing on the winds of time, and had made their empire by plundering all the civilizations which they encountered on their travels. The other reason that [17th-century] pirate dress seemed right is that it's

---

[228] Rimmer, Dave, *New Romantics: The Look*, p39.

tremendously masculine and swashbuckling, with a very strong, big silhouette – it takes the human form halfway to meet the bushy, powerful, rounded forms of the big cat.'[229]

She had neither the budget nor the time to properly reflect Christian Berard's rich costumes for Cocteau's *La Belle et la Bête* in those she designed for the Tharils but she incorporated an homage to the film into her combination of shop-bought buccaneer shirts and mock suede jackets with:

'...the embossed design on their belt buckles and cuff medallions. Crafted by June Hudson's prop maker, Roger Oldhamstead, these resin-cast emblems, sprayed gold, were far closer to the mask worn by Jean Marais in the Cocteau movie than to a straightforward bas-relief of a lion's head.'[230]

Her designs for Lalla Ward underwent a more convoluted development. She had intended to reference *La Belle et la Bête* by turning Romana into a fairy-tale prince, which would certainly have underlined the thematic connections, and 'the design included a gold-braided dress coat, a white ruffled shirt and high, knotted neck cloth, dark green velvet breeches, pale green silk stockings, grey shoes, and a waistcoat embroidered with yellow-green leaves and fastened with frog-motif buttons.'[231] However, with the prominent use of green CSO cycloramas to key the actors into the white void,

[229] Hudson, June, and Piers Britton, *Refashioning the Doctor – A 'Make-over' for a Sci-Fi Icon: Costume Design Drawings by June Hudson*, Cat.10.
[230] 'Production', *In-Vision* #50.
[231] Wiggins, *Warriors' Gate* DVD production text, episode 1.

the heavy use of green in the costume would have caused too many technical difficulties with her costume disappearing. Hudson opted instead for a Mandarin-influenced design of loose red silk jacket[232] and black trousers in keeping with the script and its own relationship with Taoism and the *I Ching*:

> 'When Romana leaves, she's going to help these rather wonderful, mystical Lion People to rebuild their civilization. [...] I saw their kingdom as a kind of Shangri-La, and so at some level I suppose I was making Romana a pilgrim. So, because she was taking on a noble, spiritualised labour, I wanted the simplicity of her dress to be total, for it to be very austere.'[233]

However, the pop video aesthetics of *Warriors' Gate* were probably more aligned with the music video accompanying the August release of David Bowie's single 'Ashes to Ashes'. A landmark, influential video, 'Ashes to Ashes' was strikingly realised in colour and black-and-white by director David Mallet and Bowie. Mallet used a mix of experimental video solarisation[234] and Quantel techniques to turn the sky black and the sea pink and segue from the surreal, hallucinatory location footage to the Expressionistic scenes recorded on the sets previously used in December 1979 for Bowie's performance of 'Space Oddity' on *The Will Kenny Everett Make It To 1980? Show*. A sequel to 'Space Oddity', 'Ashes to Ashes' depicts Bowie simultaneously as a Pierrot clown leading his followers into

---

[232] The jacket was apparently loaned from Joyce's ex-wife.

[233] Hudson, and Britton, *Refashioning the Doctor*, Cat. 9.

[234] Devereux, Eoin, Aileen Dillane and Martin Power, 'Culminating Sounds and (En)Visions – *Ashes to Ashes* and the case for Pierrot' in Devereux, Eoin, et al, eds, *David Bowie: Critical Perspectives*, p43.

oblivion before a pursuing bulldozer, a tortured asylum inmate and a withered spaceman attached to a pulsating bio-mechanical apparatus. Bowie acknowledged that he had been unintentionally inspired by the imagery of HR Giger, the Swiss surrealist designer who had provided Ridley Scott's *Alien* (1979) with its nightmarish Freudian sets and creatures.

Bowie opined that the video captured 'some feeling of nostalgia for a future. I've always been hung up on that; it creeps into everything I do, however far away I try to get from it... The idea of having seen the future of somewhere we've already been, keeps coming back to me.'[235] Uncannily, not only did his lyrics and imagery suggest Bowie was attempting to purge his career thus far by simultaneously examining his past achievements and looking to an unknown future, but he could also have been speaking about some of the ideas about precognition and synchronicity in *Warriors' Gate*. Bowie's summation of his past career and the New Romantic movement's ransacking of the past went hand-in-hand with the notion of cyclic cultural change, of history as a form of bricolage. That 'nostalgia for a future' sensibility possibly echoed Nathan-Turner's determination to take **Doctor Who** in a new direction, imbuing the series with a sense of stylistic and thematic coherence that still offered continuity with the past but unashamedly embraced what felt like the future.

---

[235] Quoted in Pegg, Nicholas, *The Complete David Bowie*, p27.

CHAPTER 6: GOING AGAINST THE GRAIN

Warriors' Gate's thematic and aesthetic components, already in situ in Gallagher's early scripts, acknowledged the impact of several French films, including work by Cocteau and Resnais, a Russian version of *Hamlet* (1964) that left a 'massive impression, never forgotten' on Gallagher from when he first saw it as a 16-year-old on a school outing organised by his English teacher[236], and a number of cult science fiction films:

> 'The ornate gardens, that was very much *Last Year at Marienbad* [1961], the Alain Resnais thing which is this weird place where […] the sun shines on some people and not on others and it's an hotel with endless corridors and a space you can't actually relate to the outside world. I also drew heavily on *Dark Star* [1974] where […] instead of a militaristic, *Forbidden Planet* [1956] kind of crew, the **Star Trek** kind of crew, where everybody was highly disciplined, […] everybody was kind of a bit unwound and a bit spacey. There were various characters in the workplace that I found a lot more true to life than the regimented, focused, heroic version of a space crew. So I kind of put that in it.'[237]

Joyce's appreciation of Resnais' *L'Année Dernière à Marienbad* had triggered his choice to direct *Warriors' Gate*. He gave the production team a sense of his approach by screening, in late July and early August 1980, Aldrich's *Kiss Me Deadly* and John Carpenter's *Dark Star*, as well as Cocteau's *Orphée* and its sequel *Le Testament*

---

[236] Gallagher, tweet to the author 24 July 2018.
[237] **Toby Hadoke's Who's Round** #166.

d'Orphée (1960). He also asked the team to watch *2001: A Space Odyssey* (1968), considering it both a philosophical and aesthetic touchstone for *Warriors' Gate*:

> 'Serious content, that's what I was trying to address. [*Warriors' Gate*] had tremendous potential within it to ask questions about the nature of the universe, what's up there, how do people live. I wanted to make it Shakespearean in that sense and that the common man is at sea in this, as [Stanley] Kubrick did with *2001*. Now, they're ambitious plans and I would never make any kind of comparison with myself and Stanley or with John Carpenter, who I think were great, great directors. Not at all. But I was ambitious enough to try and reach towards their stars. Literally, that's what I was trying to do.'[238]

In *Keep Smiling*, while Joyce's cinematic flair was shown to better effect in the filmed location material and its more impactful and expansive use of crane shots, long shots and tracking shots, the multi-camera studio work also demonstrated his visual and editorial sensibilities. It's dominated by zooms, rapid cutting between close-ups, a mix of slow and quick pans, a noir-like foregrounding of objects and faces, and an effective use of studio lighting and post-production effects to convey a growing claustrophobia and paranoia. An interesting aside is that during the dinner party scene, shot in the studio, the lead character Simon knocks over a glass of wine as he tries to tell his guests about his growing paranoia. Joyce redeploys the image in *Warriors' Gate* when the Doctor, angry at Biroc's attitude to his human servants, knocks over a goblet of wine

---

[238] **Toby Hadoke's Who's Round** #165.

during the Tharils' feast. The celebrated opening sequence of *Warriors' Gate* episode 1 is also a good example of how he expanded on this by using a set of film and television references, narratively and televisually, to underline his status as auteur.

Rolinson has already explored Joyce's opening sequence in some detail, particularly the idea that it 'doesn't just create atmosphere but also sets up a dialogue between the style and content or even between this serial's style and how **Doctor Who** usually works.' Significantly, Joyce sets out his stall immediately in terms of his televisual style, from the pull-back of the close-up on an oxygen pump, and the pan around and reverse out of the hold containing the shackled Tharils and into a corridor, to the crane shot that culminates on the privateer bridge. A countdown can be heard as the camera tracks through a corridor graffitied with 'Kilroy was here'. Joyce uses a dissolve to merge this sequence with that troublesome shot, using the handheld Ikegami, of the studio lighting grid seen up through the flooring of the set. Another dissolve returns to the corridor with the camera reversing from Royce and Aldo playing cards as the countdown falls, until it cranes up above them into the multi-level set of the bridge. It pans across Rorvik and circles around the crew, the shot then ending on a close-up of Biroc strapped into the navigation console. At this point a definite cut, to Rorvik ordering 'Hit it!' directly into camera, ends the sequence. The sequence is not a single continuous take; rather it is a series of shots linked together with a clever use of dissolves and, as Rolinson points out, 'the style makes us more aware than usual that we are being shown what we see. The function of the camera and editing is enunciative and authorial, as exploring physical space takes priority over establishing narrative space.'[239] However, these two minutes and 22 seconds also create several intertextual perspectives on the narrative.

Firstly, they introduce us to the privateer, one of three televisual environments in *Warriors' Gate* coherently established in Gallagher's early drafts, and the end of the sequence reveals Biroc as the link to the banqueting hall at the gateway that will, in turn, provide a portal into the monochrome world of the Tharil palace and gardens. Secondly, the camera's exploration of the interior of the privateer, as Rolinson notes, rests only to introduce Biroc in close-up. It's here that the cyclic narrative of *Warriors' Gate* both begins and ends, with him on screen as the countdown reaches zero and after the camera deliberately seeks him out as the narrative's symbol of predestination. Gallagher's first drafts may open very differently from the rehearsal and camera scripts but his original proposition, of shifting from negative into positive numbers to demarcate the tipping point between E-Space and N-Space, is present here. The countdown reaching zero also represents the zero coordinates locked off by Biroc in the TARDIS to indicate the intersection between the two. The serial's narrative is also bookended with scenes of the crew assembled on the bridge. In episode 1 they attempt to escape a time rift and land in the void and in episode 4 they attempt to back-blast through the gateway. Finally, the camera travelling through the vertical plane up into the bridge establishes the hierarchies between the crew and the Tharils, even though the relationship between them is ambiguous at this point. It demarcates the space in terms of the ship's command structure, contrasting the

---

[239] Rolinson, '(Times and) Spaces of Television'.

lazy maintenance men Royce and Aldo, nonchalantly playing cards in the vandalised bowels of the ship, with the tension of the countdown overseen on the bridge by Rorvik and Packard. Biroc's presence there not only reinforces the restriction and abuse of the Tharils but also underlines their value to the crew, particularly his importance in previsualising the privateer's fateful encounter with the TARDIS.

It has been suggested this sequence resembles the opening of *Alien*, where Ridley Scott's camera prowls around the empty corridors of the mining ship *Nostromo* before the crew are woken from hypersleep. There are echoes in Joyce's work but *Alien* isn't the de facto inspiration. Scott establishes the mood with a series of reverse tracks, pans, short takes and specific cuts as opposed to Joyce's crane shots, dissolves or fades. Scott's film shares with *Warriors' Gate* the sense of an industrial, battered environment expressed in a combination of production design (Ron Cobb designed both *Alien* and *Dark Star*), lighting and camera moves. Joyce's use of the studio lights filtering through the metal flooring of the set (built of salvaged metal pallets from *Alien*) is the clearest acknowledgement of Scott's aesthetic. Joyce wanted a realistic depiction of working on a spaceship and while Scott shows the *Nostromo*'s crew eating, drinking and smoking as they argue about their abrupt wake-up call, Joyce's sense of realism probably originated from Gallagher's descriptive scripts and the influence of *Dark Star*. The crew quarters are squalid in *Dark Star*, a riot of porn pin-ups, graffiti, discarded food and some unsavoury-looking garments hanging across the space, and the bridge is extremely cramped. The unkempt, anxious crew face a dehumanising daily routine dulled only by muzak, playing cards, drinking and smoking.

Gallagher similarly describes the privateer as a damaged ship that's dirty, rusting, barely held together or flightworthy, and the crew's habits, where 'beyond the helmsman's position a line has been rigged, and a greasy old set of what looks like one-piece underwear is hanging to dry.'[240] A signifier of the entropic ethos of season 18, where 'the more you keep putting things together, the more they keep falling apart'[241], the production design of the privateer corridors uses the 'Kilroy was here'[242] graffiti as an in-joke because a crew member called Kilroy does appear later in the episode. Taking his lead from *Dark Star* and *Alien*, Joyce wanted to show the privateer crew smoking pot, but even when he capitulated to the use of tobacco he was refused this embellishment for fear that it would promote smoking to younger viewers[243]. *Alien*, like *Dark Star*, also explores the hierarchies and power relationships between crew members and, like those of the privateer, the *Nostromo*'s engineers Brett and Parker are concerned about how their perilous circumstances will affect their bonuses. In *Warriors' Gate*, Rorvik upbraids the crew about their bonuses and in episode 2 Aldo and Royce acknowledge they're on 'the all-in contract' that won't affect their bonus if they bungle the revival of a Tharil. Further visual parity with Carpenter's film is found in the standard costume design for the

---

[240] Hull Archives. Gallagher, 'The Dream Time' episode 1, p14-15.

[241] Rolinson, '(Times and) Spaces of Television'.

[242] The use of the slogan perhaps dates back to around 1937 when Second World War American servicemen used it to flag the places in which they were stationed.

[243] **Toby Hadoke's Who's Round** #165. Oddly, this was deemed acceptable in 1984 when the crew of the dilapidated space station in *Resurrection of the Daleks* was depicted smoking on screen.

privateer's crew, referred to in the costume and makeup plot for *Warriors' Gate* as 'one utilitarian costume of working clothes, similar to those depicted in *Dark Star*, with the addition of name tags and identity photographs.' Rorvik and Packard's costumes were also differentiated by additional insignia, 'indicating greater rank or status than the rest of the crew.'[244] Costume designer June Hudson used genuine NASA engineers' overalls as the base for each crew member but specifically designed and made Rorvik's costume[245].

Joyce has acknowledged that the inspiration for his opening sequence was the single continuous take that opened Orson Welles' film noir thriller *Touch of Evil* (1958). Welles' sequence starts with a close-up of a bomb and timer mechanism, the camera pulls back and follows a bomber, who plants it in the boot of a car. Welles' camera cranes up for a bird's eye perspective of the car as two people get into it. For three minutes, the camera swoops around a building and, reverse tracking, it follows the car through crowded streets. It drops down to pick out the two main characters of the film, Mike Vargas and his wife Susie, walking along as the car drives out of shot. The camera reverse tracks with them to a checkpoint at the US-Mexican border where the car draws up beside them (it's a film, like *La Belle et la Bête* and *Orphée*, depicting the borderline between two distinct worlds). They walk out of shot as the female passenger in the car says she can hear a ticking noise in her head and the car drives off. The camera then returns to Vargas and his wife as they embrace and kiss. This single take abruptly ends when the car explodes. In

---

[244] BBC WAC file T65/169/1, *Warriors' Gate*. Costume and makeup plots, 20 August 1980.
[245] Wiggins, *Warriors' Gate* DVD production text, episode 1.

Warriors' Gate, for the unseen but present threat of the ticking bomb, Joyce substituted the voiceover countdown, the close-up of the oxygen pump mirrored the close-up of the bomb, and Welles' reverse tracking and crane shot was matched in Joyce's reverse from the hold into the corridor and the crane shot from the hold and up into the bridge. Like the shot of the car exploding that dramatically puts a full stop to Welles' uninterrupted take, Rorvik's order to camera as the countdown hits zero punctuates Joyce's sequence.

The opening sequence represents Joyce's response to the script in visual and narrative terms, not only as a director but also as a writer, and it's easy to forget that he and Bidmead had significant input on paper before recording even began. During an era where the producer-writer relationship was often a privileged one, it was also unusual in **Doctor Who** for a director to be so invested in the script. This was dictated by the circumstances of the production but, for example, producer Barry Letts' agreement with the BBC allowed him to direct one serial per season, including *Planet of the Spiders* (1974), of which he was the uncredited co-writer with Robert Sloman. Director Michael Hayes also made an uncredited contribution to the scripts for *City of Death*. It could, however, be argued that Joyce was the first director on **Doctor Who** whose authorial contribution to a serial's conception and production was so demonstrable. He believed that:

> '...most directors worth their salt should write their material or co-author their material. I don't believe you can really be a true auteur without an input in the script, which is what of course those wonderful American directors that we know as great names would do as a matter of course. I mean, what I

did with **Doctor Who** was not unusual in the Hollywood scenario.'[246]

Joyce saw his control of the material as akin to a tradition stretching back to writer-directors like Billy Wilder, John Huston, Orson Welles and Francis Ford Coppola, and one still practised today by the likes of Joel and Ethan Cohen, Paul Thomas Anderson and Christopher Nolan. In television, he was also following in the footsteps of directors, including those who worked on **Doctor Who**, who 'remain critcally neglected' in favour of the producer-writer hierarchy[247].

Joyce's control of the material also incorporates specific visual styles, initially inspired by the film noir visual etiquette of *Touch of Evil* and, later, by Aldrich's *Kiss Me Deadly*. Aldrich's amalgam of high and low angles, framing through foreground positioning of faces, bodies and objects, a depth of field allowing the viewer to get a sense of real space, and the use of long takes and sequences are stylistic, three-dimensional touches that Joyce imports into *Warriors' Gate*. This sense of depth and space can be seen in the shots on the privateer bridge during Rorvik's interrogation of Biroc when the Tharil fails to visualise the ship's warp jump. The camera shifts focus between them, the scene gaining depth as Biroc becomes the point of interest and it culminates with big close-ups, using the Ikegami camera, of both of them as Rorvik makes demands of Biroc. This depth of field is further exploited when Joyce uses Quantel and inlay to depict the spinning coin sent into the air by Aldo and Royce, landing and spinning to a halt in the foreground as one of the bridge consoles burns in the background. A jump cut from the spinning coin is

---

[246] **Toby Hadoke's Who's Round** #167.
[247] Rolinson, '"**Who** done it"', p185.

matched to a similarly pixelated image of the TARDIS spinning on the monitor screen above Biroc's head. Joyce zooms into Biroc's eye, offering a mind's eye focus on the revolving image of the TARDIS using Quantel and, in a lovely moment of illusion within illusion, a balsa wood model of the TARDIS treated electronically to represent a digital wireframe image of the police box. Within a matter of minutes, Joyce has used a handheld camera, pedestal cameras on a crane, videographics and practical effects to expand and compress the space between characters, altering the depth of field with camera focus, movement, jump cuts and video effects. This was unusual for **Doctor Who** and again underlines Joyce's determination to put his own stamp on the episodes.

Narratively, the scene is also important because the 'philosophy' of *Warriors' Gate* becomes an adjunct to Joyce's techniques. It accrues a thematic depth, presenting Biroc's visualisation as an allusion to David Bohm's theory of the implicate order of the universe, the aboriginal concept of the Dreaming and the notion that order can be determined out of the apparent randomness of an *I Ching* divination or a spinning coin. Biroc's visualisation depends on an indivisible connection between the observer and the observed, and it corresponds with Jung's view, in his introduction to Richard Wilhelm's 1950 edition of the *I Ching*, that synchronicity takes 'the coincidence of the events in space and time as meaning something more than mere chance, namely a peculiar interdependence of objective events among themselves as well as with the subjective (psychic) state of the observer or observers.'

Bohm's theory in the *Sunday Times* article that Bidmead sent to Gallagher also explained how the subatomic particles of the universe are viewed as disconnected from one another because only a portion of their reality can be seen. Biroc knows that the observed image of the TARDIS and the reality of the TARDIS, like those seemingly separate subatomic particles, are connected. Bohm theorised that at a deeper level reality is a hologram in which the past, present, and future all exist simultaneously and that at some point it might even be possible to reach into this holographic level of reality and visualise the past or the future. Biroc sees the past, present and future simultaneously, possessing the ability to tune into certain frequencies within a universal holographic consciousness, where seemingly strange synchronicities and random events may, in the end, be completely determined on a subatomic, spacetime holographic level. This suggests that the implicate order is like the Aboriginal Dreamtime where 'our dreaming self is deeper in the psyche than our conscious self – and thus closer to the primal ocean in which past, present and future become one – and it may be easier for it to access information about the future.' [248] Biroc understands events have already been determined when he sees the TARDIS in the continuum. Joyce, as Rolinson notes, creates a tension between visual style and narrative within this scene, primarily to emphasise Biroc as the still point and origin of the story:

> 'Firstly, the dynamic style has accompanied nothing happening, but as the camera stops and we see the character who will do nothing, things start to happen (the story). Secondly, Rorvik is having trouble getting Biroc to visualise,

---

[248] Talbot, Michael, *The Holographic Universe* (1991), p210. Talbot explores the implicate order and the holographic universe theories, and Bohm's collaboration with neuroscientist Karl Pribam and their theory that the brain is actually a holographic storage network.

but perhaps the first few minutes of the story are all about visualisation, Joyce's and Biroc's.'

This occurs to the Doctor in the TARDIS scene that follows. In frustration, Romana utters 'we've got to do something' when the TARDIS fails to respond to their control, but the Doctor contemplates, 'Have we?' If they do nothing then perhaps that will facilitate their escape from E-Space. They discuss the use of random sampling, mentioning the *I Ching*, to determine a path through E-Space. While the Doctor sees this as part of an holistic view of the universe, very much in tune with Bohm's theory, Romana dismisses it as mystical superstition and 'Astral Jung'. Adric's casting of the *I Ching* hexagram 'the taming power of the small' is a response to the Doctor and Romana's unease at subconsciously trying to 'generate non-determinate action.' This brings Biroc, who initiates the start and end point of the story, to the TARDIS. However, it's also possible to draw comparisons with Joyce's own experiences at Television Centre, using the studio space to visualise what he felt was likely to happen with the convergence of television and film. As Rolinson so eloquently states:

> 'The studio is the perfect place for the opening of *Warriors' Gate*: a transitional, liminal space, full of tensions. Past (a form of drama from which Joyce and television wanted to escape), present (the video studio's present-tense immediacy) and future (or lack thereof).'[249]

Several scenes articulate this tension, as Joyce pushes the immediacy of the television studio to create his own cinematic sense

---

[249] Rolinson, '(Times and) Spaces of Television'.

of space, realism and thematic resonance. Aldrich's film noir stylisation informs the framing of bodies, shooting through sections of the set and using characters and objects close to the foreground to underline the relationship between the crew and their environment. In episode 1, Joyce slowly zooms through the ship's damaged infrastructure to a close-up on Lane relaying the status of the engines back to Rorvik, emphasising depth and space through abstraction.

This abstraction is repeated in episode 4. Lazlo's electrocution of Sagan, where Joyce cuts from their struggle, shot with handheld camera, to a close-up of a sparking contact on Sagan's chest, ends graphically with an abrupt cut to and brief zoom in on Sagan's face dropping into frame, mouth open and eyes rolled back. The close-up of Sagan's inverted face prompts allusions to the camera pulling out from Welles' inverted face in the opening of his *Othello* (1951) and the skewed angle on Anthony Perkins' face in his expressionistic version of Kafka's *The Trial* (1962). Of more relevance is a reference to a shot of Jean Marais as the dead Orpheus lying on the back seat of a car in Cocteau's *Orphée*. Joyce's insertion of this shot is not a decorative addition. It's a jump-scare that borrows from the horror genre, simultaneously arresting the viewer and implying that the reality of the privateer's world has been turned upside down and its crew are about to enter death's dominion.

Rorvik is often seen looming threateningly over his crew and, particularly in episode 4, over the Doctor in the ship's hold before their violent struggle. At first, Rorvik's splayed legs act as a frame within which the Doctor appears, then Joyce cuts to an extreme low angle of Rorvik, in silhouette, bearing down on the Doctor. Their dispute is played back and forth using these two shots until the

Doctor is pushed to the floor. Before he cuts to the fight proper, Joyce emphasises the power struggle with a camera positioned under the grilled flooring as Rorvik tries to strangle the Doctor with his own scarf. Repeating his earlier visual motif, Joyce first shows the Doctor's inverted face as he recovers and the camera then rises up to frame Biroc. After Biroc rescues Romana and the Doctor and implores them to 'do nothing', the scene culminates with Rorvik looking into camera and berating the absent Doctor. His line, 'I'm sick of your kind, faint-hearted, do-nothing, lily-livered dead weights. This is the end for all of you. I'm finally getting something done,' ends with a triumphant cackle but it also juxtaposes the two philosophies – rational action and metaphysical instinct – at the heart of the story.

Biroc has convinced the Doctor that doing 'the right sort of nothing' is the appropriate reaction to the situation. This proposition evokes Eastern philosophy, where 'the structures and phenomena we observe in nature are nothing but creations of our measuring and categorising mind,' and this surface level of reality will dissolve away 'if this state is transcended.' [250] In Taoist philosophy this transcendence is known as the wu-wei, 'a term which means literally "non-action"' and the Doctor refrains from inappropriate action because, according to Taoism's originator Lao Tzu, '"by non-action, everything can be done."' [251] Rorvik believes his frustration with events will only be resolved through drastic action, using a back-blast, whatever cost. Taking his cue from Gallagher's themes about the impact of technology on the fragility of human

---

[250] Capra, *The Tao of Physics*, p306.
[251] Capra, *The Tao of Physics*, pp129-30.

subjectivity, Joyce explores Rorvik's sense of reality and rationality in certain scenes and underlines his growing paranoia.

Actor Clifford Rose alluded to this, believing Rorvik resembled Arthur Lowe's equally frustrated Captain Mainwaring from **Dad's Army** (1968-1978): 'They are both figures of authority trying to keep together a bunch of men to do a certain job and not being entirely effective. He had a kind of story, a personal story, a development and I can see it was leading somewhere fairly extreme.'[252] However, there are several other layers to this sense of frustration. Perhaps Joyce saw in Rorvik's cry of triumph that surreal, Beckettian moment he first saw on film where a man smashes his expensive radiogram simply because he couldn't stop it playing. While Gallagher may have used Biroc to vent his own discontent while working for Granada, in Joyce's struggle to get the story to the screen it's tempting to say he too was 'finally getting something done' by going against the grain of production etiquette and had thus 'complicated the director's place within the 'creative power relations' of the programme.'[253]

In episode 2, when Romana has her cryptic conversation with Packard, Lane and Rorvik outside the TARDIS, not only does Joyce use another long take to evoke a sense of realism but he also uses to his advantage the compromises agreed with Nathan-Turner during production. Rather than circle the actors with the camera or cut to them from one camera to another, Joyce choreographs them and uses the handheld Ikegami to follow their dialogue and movement in a single take. This reflects the handheld camerwork associated with a realism that had infiltrated Hollywood in the 1960s, inspired

---

[252] Rose, Clifford, 'The Dreaming'.
[253] Rolinson, '"**Who** done it"', p186.

by the documentaries and cinema of the French New Wave. The camera is centred on Lalla Ward as she weaves between Rose and Kenneth Cope and delivers her lines. Rose, Cope and David Kincaid follow a series of cues to come in from frame left and right as they exchange lines with her. Kincaid moves from left to right in the background and the blocking of the scene ensures he's in shot as the camera moves with Ward and the others. It's an expedient way of covering the scene and it uses the physical movement of actors, together with their dialogue, to create a relationship between the deterministic world of the privateer crew and Romana's growing sense that the missing Biroc represents a different reality. He's a Tharil whose whereabouts pose 'an interesting philosophical question', given her reference to Bohm's 'implicate theory' when she asks the crew about their means of travel.

The handheld single take confers a sense of verisimilitude to these scenes and, even though it's a stylistic cinematic device with no cuts for roughly two minutes, it feels like the viewer particpates in the scene. According to Joyce, it got a reaction from Nathan-Turner:

> 'He didn't know how I'd rehearsed it. I said, "OK we'll shoot it," you know. We got it in one take and he said, "Fuck me, that's three and half minutes." I said, "Yes, that's it, move on." I thought, if you want to take it in one I can do it. Give me a bit of rehearsal time and I can do it. So I was adapting to the circumstances, I think, pretty quickly.'

These circumstances were presumably Joyce's untenable pace of production that Dixon had mentioned in his report, where he claimed Joyce was working at the much slower shooting ratio of a feature film. Responding to these concerns and Nathan-Turner's

143

request to speed up his rehearsals, Joyce believed he could compromise, recover lost time, ensure he had enough coverage, and 'sort of had my own back, in a way, by doing long takes.'[254] This can also be seen in Joyce's deep-space staging, another hallmark of Welles and Kubrick and often related to single camera technique, of several scenes in episode 2. In particular, these include the shot of Lazlo's electrocuted body, shown in the foreground as Aldo and Joyce attempt to revive him, that ends with a zoom in onto his smoking claw (itself a nod to the Beast in *La Belle et la Bête*); the POV handheld work on the bridge as Lazlo stalks Romana; and the striking sense of depth as Rorvik and his party enter the banqueting hall at the far end of the set as, in the foreground, the Doctor interrogates the Gundan about the gateway.

Finally, Joyce's handling of both the monochrome tour of the Tharil palace and gardens and the climactic banqueting hall sequence in episode 3 expand on his film technique and have thematic and televisual resonances with *L'Année Dernière à Marienbad*.

A collaboration between French director Resnais and avant-garde novelist Alain Robbe-Grillet, *Marienbad* was filmed on location at a number of baroque palaces in Germany and its interiors were completed at the Photosonor studios in Paris. Resnais created the palace and gardens of Marienbad by collaging together several locations. As Robbe-Grillet observed, Marienbad as a real place 'is no longer on any map' and the characters' recollections of spending last year there are a hallucination. The gateway in *Warriors' Gate* also has no map reference, 'exists' at zero coordinates and can only

---

[254] **Toby Hadoke's Who's Round** #165.

be reached by visualising it in the mind's eye. *Marienbad*'s 'baroque palace overlooking expansive, ornate, frozen gardens'[255] delineates interior and exterior space just as distinctly as the separation between privateer and gateway, and between banqueting hall and black-and-white gardens. *Marienbad* is also an existential conundrum where a man, known only as X, tries to persuade a woman, A, that he knows her from the affair they had there last year. A at first rejects the possibility of the affair and her previous knowledge of X, but then gradually begins to doubt herself as the film plays with time, space, memory and identity. It's a claustrophobic fantasy dominated by slow, seemingly endless tracking shots (perhaps another influence on episode 1's opening sequence) of corridors festooned with roccoco décor and formal gardens lined with topiary and statues. In the film's play on memory and time the palace's other guests echo the main characters' dialogue and repeat stories of events from the past and the present.

Gallagher's first draft script picks up on *Marienbad*'s influence, and a sense of a world frozen in time, of a history stalled, with the Doctor's arrival in the palace gardens where 'the greenery and stonework all appear to have been dusted with a light frost.'[256] Joyce's combination of black-and-white photographs of Powis Castle and Scene Sync effects to bring the colour images of the Doctor and Romana into this world effectively replicate Gallagher's own ideas and aspects of *Marienbad*'s crisp monochrome cinematography.

---

[255] Wilson, Emma, *French Film Directors: Alain Resnais*, p68.
[256] Hull Archives. Gallagher, 'The Dream Time', episode 3, p13.

Joyce believed the strength of the images came from how objects 'stand, how they look and present themselves and I think photography is very good at capturing that. And that's what I wanted, I wanted that feeling of history. I wanted to bring that quality into a studio where everyone's talking about colour.'[257] Furthermore, the images of travelling through mirrors to other universes in the past, present and future in *Warriors' Gate*, a nod to Cocteau's *Orphée*, find their analogue in Resnais' film:

> '...the mansion Resnais creates is encrusted with many mirrors in whose crystalline, reflective surfaces we see much of the action [...] which encompasses a real image and its mirrored reflection, in such a way that the relation between the two, actual and virtual, is drawn into question.'[258]

This idea of virtual and actual recollection relates to the way the banqueting hall displays a key moment in Tharil history, which 'moves from slavery to enslavement to redemption, like the rise and fall and rise again of a civilisation bound to the wheel of history.'[259] Throughout *Warriors' Gate*, Biroc represents this cycle as a semblance of the past, the present and the future, one that determines the fate of the Tharils and the humans. This fate is constructed from a repetition of images, the 'shadow of my past and your future' illustrated by the mirrors and time slippage between the banqueting halls, visually connected by the falling of an axe and the knocking over of a goblet. Just as *Marienbad*'s characters must

---

[257] Joyce, 'The Dreaming'.
[258] Wilson, *Alain Resnais*, p12.
[259] Burk, Graeme, and Robert Smith?, *Who's 50: The 50 Doctor Who Stories to Watch Before You Die – An Unofficial Companion*, p208.

interpret the troubling and often confusing amalgam of their own past and present memories, the Tharils similarly deal with the abusive relationships they and the slavers have foisted upon one another. *Warriors' Gate* relates this in a non-linear fashion, as similarly in *Marienbad*, 'the viewer remains uncertain whether images we see represent actual events, remembered events or indeed fantasised events' and Resnais articulates a formal concern with 'fate, chance and plural destinies.'[260]

Joyce's dynamic synchronisation of two scenes in the banqueting hall, where past and present destinies gradually mesh together, suggests a deeper reality as, in the present, Rorvik holds his crew at gunpoint over their lunch and demands that they find a way through the mirrors and, in the past, the Doctor witnesses the Gundan attack on the Tharil feast. The timeslip between the two banqueting halls is achieved when Joyce cuts between several zooms on Romana's reaction, with history playing out virtually in her mind's eye and then reoccurring in real time. Like the viewer, she is, initially, a spectator and then becomes a witness to the Doctor (appropriately) doing nothing. An axe is seen hitting the table twice – before and after the Gundans burst into the room – implying she foresees or dreams the attack and then is actually present by the Doctor's side.

Joyce first achieves a sense of shifting time with an elegant crane shot, reversing out of a close-up on the Doctor as he watches the feast from the minstrels' gallery, panning across the candlelit set and then zooming in to the table toward a roast on a serving dish. The roast vanishes and is replaced by a dusty, empty dish. The camera retraces its move and zooms in on Romana and Lazlo standing in the

---

[260] Wilson, *Alain Resnais*, pp12-13.

same position in the old banqueting hall. Joyce cuts in the shot of the axe falling. The scene with Rorvik and his men continues, and they see Romana and Lazlo escape through the mirror. The Doctor attends the feast, but it is then disturbed by the arrival of the Gundans. Joyce zooms in to Romana, now on the other side of the mirror and in the same position in the minstrels' gallery, and cuts to the robots bursting into the room. The axe is embedded in the table in the past and then matched with a close-up on the cobwebbed axe in the present to further emphasise the abrupt shift in time as Rorvik welcomes the Doctor and Romana's sudden reappearance in his timeline. While Harper did set up and direct some of these scenes under Joyce's supervision, it's Joyce's editing that reflects Resnais' jarring use of montage and cutting in *Marienbad* to suggest moving in time and space or the juxtaposition of memories. It's an editing dynamic that would dominate commercials and music videos. Renowned film editor Walter Murch believed audiences came to accept this style of intercutting 'because it resembles the way images are juxtaposed in our dreams. In fact, the abruptness of the cut may be one of the key determinants in actually producing the similarity between films and dreams.'[261] It's notable that Murch's perspectives on editing reflect Joyce's own view that films can 'depict a mental state or a state of enhanced reality or remembrance in a way that we recall things in our own minds.'[262]

The juxtaposition of the two banqueting hall scenes, completed on a single set redressed to reflect the different periods in which the

---

[261] Murch, Walter, *In the Blink of an Eye: A Perspective on Film Editing*, p58.
[262] Joyce, interview with author.

action takes place, also reflects the tensions ingrained in the production process when 'several shots from the new banqueting hall were taped onto a video cassette so that they could be lined up exactly with shots to be made the following day on the old banqueting hall set.'[263] An efficient way to line up specific shots of the empty roast dish and the axe in the table and achieve accurate continuity between the two sequences, this televisual layering of images also provides another tantalising allusion to Bohm's theory. Just as the observer of the fish on the television screen understands something of the deeper reality and connectedness to the image being observed, the two recordings of new and old banqueting hall, using the cassette recording as a virtual bookmark, emanate from one source: a set in the television studio. The production of the final images describes, in the parlance of quantum theory, 'a complicated web of relations between the various parts of a unified whole'[264].

This sense of a fictional world within a television world is heightened further with the televisual realisation of Gallagher's white void. The deeper reality, from a production standpoint, is that scenes were shot against a green cyclorama and the void was inlaid from a locked-off camera trained on 'the inside of a large, bracket-mounted perspex hemisphere, provided by Effects, which had been spray-painted an off-white grey.'[265] As with much of *Warriors' Gate*, the viewer understands what is finally produced on screen by observing the deeper reality hidden beneath it, narratively and visually.

---

[263] *Doctor Who: The Complete History*, Volume 33, p65.
[264] Capra, *The Tao of Physics*, p150.
[265] 'Production', *In-Vision* #50.

CHAPTER 7: 'THE IMPECCABLE REALISM OF UNREALITY'

In episode 1, Biroc's slow-motion emergence into the TARDIS from the time winds also marries the televisual and videographic with Joyce's first proper visual reference to Cocteau's *La Belle et la Bête*. Cocteau's work had a significant impact on Gallagher's scripts and *La Belle et la Bête* was the sine qua non for his depiction of the Tharils, the gateway, and the palace and gardens beyond the mirrors in the banqueting hall. Not only do Cocteau's films and Gallagher's scripts provide Joyce with further cinematic associations, in terms of visual intertextuality, but also the structure of *La Belle et la Bête* influences the differentiation between the realism of the privateer and the dream like, poetic world of the Tharils and the gateway.

The problems Cocteau himself experienced during the making of *La Belle et la Bête* between August 1945 and June 1946 eerily reflect the pitfalls Joyce encountered in the studio. Cocteau struggled to find money and resources in post-Liberation France. He secured finance from an independent producer, who kept a tight rein on the film's budget, to bring his version of Madame Le Prince de Beaumont's celebrated fairy-tale to the screen[266].

Cocteau suffered the combined onslaught of illness, power cuts, union action that halted set construction and filming, injuries to

---

[266] Given the context of authorship in this book, it is interesting that de Beaumont published her tale in 1756 but it was actually a rewritten, shortened version of the much longer story published by the French novelist Madame Gabrielle de Villeneuve in 1740. Variations of the tale have existed for thousands of years.

actors that necessitated changes in schedule or the use of stand-ins, and aircraft noise ruining takes on location. He was hospitalised halfway through production. Film stock, difficult to source in post-war France, often failed to reproduce the crisp, black-and-white chiaroscuro of his cinematographer Henri Alekan. Alekan had put aside his standard approach and acceded to Cocteau's demand for a documentary style that captured 'the impeccable realism of unreality', inspired by the Dutch masters Rembrandt and Vermeer for the domestic scenes set at the merchant's farmhouse and by the engravings of Gustave Doré for the magical realm of the Beast's castle[267]. Cocteau's request that the poetic, traditionally expressed in cinematic soft focus, be rendered in such a contradictory fashion echoes Joyce's own struggles to stretch the boundaries of the television studio.

Billy Smart's exploration of Cocteau's inspiration, 'integral to the visual and philosophical construction of the world of *Warriors' Gate*', prioritises Gallagher's authorial stamp and his use of Cocteau:

> 'Firstly, to form impossible connections between parallel worlds and realities [...] that can often be formulated as representing dream or unconscious states for those who cross between them [...] The second lesson that Gallagher takes from Cocteau is the application of the topography of *La Belle et la Bête* to create an imaginative fantastical world, governed by its own rules and logic.'[268]

---

[267] Williams, James S, *French Film Directors: Jean Cocteau*, p66-67.
[268] Smart, Billy, '**Doctor Who**: *Warriors' Gate* (1981), Jean Cocteau and the Realm of Videographic Fantasy'.

It suggests a narrative in line with the philosophical aspects of the morality tale that Bidmead retrospectively saw as his remit rather than one determined by 'pure science'. The combined influence of New Wave science fiction, fairy-tale, and quantum theory certainly complicated Bidmead's view that stories should be scientifically rational and understandable. Joyce's first image of the smoke-enshrouded Biroc underlines Cocteau's entreaty in the opening of *La Belle et la Bête*, asking the adult audience to embrace the fairy-tale he offers them and a child's belief 'in the smoking hands of a man-beast who kills.'[269] It could be said that **Doctor Who** has requested this of its whole audience since 1963, and Gallagher and Joyce similarly embrace the concerns of fairy-tale, myth and legend with 'social harmony, the overcoming of social problems and the defeat of cultural adversaries.'[270] To initiate this, Gallagher has Biroc guide the TARDIS and its occupants to the void and the gateway, just as Cocteau draws his merchant through the misty forest towards the Beast's enchanted castle. Biroc's appearance proper then aligns to the Beast's full reveal to the merchant and cements the intertextual marriage between *Warriors' Gate* and Cocteau's film. Cocteau describes the Beast as:

> '...a lord in fashionable court dress, having nothing of the animal to him but the head and the hands. His head is a magnificent animal's head, a sort of lion with clear eyes. His muzzle glistens in the sun. His hands are a man's hands, hairy

---

[269] Cocteau's written introduction opens *La Belle et la Bête*.
[270] Jones, Steven Swann, *The Fairy Tale: The Magic Mirror of the Imagination*, p16.

and tipped with claws. His open shirt exposes a dark fleece.'[271]

In Gallagher's first draft script, Biroc is:

'...tall and broad-shouldered, basically human in form although his features are leonine; his hands are broad paws held in a permanent clawed curve, and what shows of his face, head and chest is covered with a tawny-gold fur which is swept back in a mane reaching just below his collar. His ears are high and pointed, his mouth wide and showing the tiny points of fangs at its corners; he's dressed very plainly, in a baggy white swashbuckler's shirt with open collar and brown pants tucked into turned-over boots. The shirt is torn and stained in a couple of places – he might be on the run from a fairy-tale.'[272]

In the castle grounds, Cocteau reveals the Beast in full profile before swooping in for a close-up when he accuses the merchant of stealing his roses and barks his demands before vanishing into the undergrowth. Equally mysterious, Biroc takes control of the TARDIS, warns its crew about those who follow him and magically disappears back into the void. The Beast's first appearance in *La Belle et la Bête* is also the first imprint upon it of the fantastical. Before this Cocteau used the verisimilitude of Rembrandt and Vermeer to inform the documentary realism of the merchant scraping a living in a humble farmhouse with his three daughters and their servants. It is a naturalistic and often comic interpretation of Beauty's two spoilt

---

[271] Cocteau, Jean, *Beauty and the Beast: Scenario and Dialogs*, ed Robert M Hammond, shot 96, pp92-94.
[272] Hull Archives. Gallagher, 'The Dream Time', episode 1, p10.

sisters, her brother and his friend Avenant. Cocteau contrasts the realism of the merchant's farmhouse, its squabbling family and their everyday activities such as washing, eating and cleaning, with the magical, in which Beauty meets the Beast in his enchanted castle, where statues come to life and an age-old curse waits to be lifted. The magical gradually infiltrates the domestic realm when Beauty is allowed to use a magic mirror to see her ailing father and a glove to instantly return to the farmhouse. Similarly, fantasy and realism are also in flux in *Warriors' Gate* and there is, like Cocteau's film, a split between rationalism and magic, between the interior space of the privateer, with its day-to-day grind akin to the working environs of the farmhouse, and the bizarre space outside where the Beast's castle is represented by the void, the gateway and the gardens beyond the mirrors.

Visual references, in terms of the design of the entrance and banqueting hall interior of the gateway, initially cleave to Gallagher's descriptions that were inspired by *La Belle et la Bête*. As Smart acknowledges, 'the Doctor's initial arrival at the castle acts as both a quotation from – and a discourse with – the moment in the film when Beauty's father arrives in the mansion of the Beast.'[273] After panning away from a close-up of the dysfunctional Gundans, Joyce establishes the cobwebbed interior of the banqueting hall by using the mirror next to the robots as a frame, reflecting a large portion of the studio set in deep focus. This is the first shot showing the mirror and, at first, it appears like a doorway into the set rather than the camera capturing a reflection of it. Its eventual narrative function as a portal to another world is only confirmed after Joyce shows Biroc

---

[273] Smart, 'Jean Cocteau and the Realm of Videographic Fantasy'.

passing through it. Joyce heralds the Doctor's arrival with a close-up of an overturned goblet, then he briefly pans to some skeletal remains (more symbols of decay) and follows the Doctor to the table, where he sets the goblet back up. After straightening the dusty, immobile Gundans, he examines Biroc's discarded manacles by the mirror, unaware that one of the reactivated Gundans is stalking him.

Like the Beast's enchanted castle, the banqueting hall is guarded by seemingly inanimate figures that suddenly spring into life. The goblet, filled with wine and offered to the affrighted merchant by disembodied hands in Cocteau's film, is initially discarded on the table but is the first thing the Doctor attends to. It is a subtle visual acknowledgement of the importance of the banqueting hall to the narrative, with the goblet as a marker of the intersection between its past, present and future. When the Doctor sets the goblet back up he is unconsciously responding to an action he took in the banqueting hall beyond the mirror and during the past glories of the Tharils' empire. Again, there is a sense of tuning into a holographic reality where, for the characters and the audience, the past, present and future are happening simultaneously within the story, a sensation that Joyce returns to with spectacular effect in episode 3's cliffhanger.

The Doctor's encounter with the Gundans is not only a riff on the living sculptures and the candlelit interiors of the Beast's castle but also recognises elements of Grigori Kozintsev's film adaptation of *Hamlet*, the one that left a lasting impression on Gallagher. One of the most striking scenes in Kozintsev's majestic film is Hamlet's first encounter with the ghost of his recently dead father on the castle battlements. The ghost appears in silhouette with its cloak streaming in the wind and Hamlet, also in silhouette in the distance, pursues it through the Gothic arches of the castle. The imposing castle, shot on location at the fortress of Ivangorod, is the equal to Cocteau in terms of its impetus on Gallagher's setting of the banqueting hall and his first draft descriptions in episodes 1 and 2 of the hall's passageways and minstrels' gallery. Ivangorod and the Beast's castle also feed into Graeme Story's set for *Warriors' Gate*, with its iron candelabras, stone vaults and lion statues, and into the Gothic imagery of the gateway when it is seen in full, as a model shot, in episode 3. When Hamlet comes face to face with the ghost, at first a seemingly empty suit of armour that jerkily advances in slow motion toward the camera, it visually recalls the Gundan waking up and attacking the Doctor. The Doctor's escape from Rorvik in episode 2, disappearing behind the upper arches of Story's multi-level banqueting hall set, is reminiscent of Hamlet's silhouette pursuing the ghost through the castle arches.

Cocteau's fantasy continues to resonate in episode 2 when the revived but injured Lazlo makes his way to the bridge. Joyce's POV shot of the unseen Tharil and Romana's reaction to his threatening approach recalls Beauty's first encounter with the Beast. Joyce's interpretation of that **Doctor Who** standard, the unveiling of the monster, reinforces the notion that the monstrous in *Warriors' Gate* is not what it seems. Joyce switches between two POVs – Lazlo's and Romana's – by using matching handheld shots. Lazlo's POV and his staggered breathing on the soundtrack build tension as the Tharil climbs the gangway to the bridge and Joyce intercuts this with Romana's close-up reactions. On the bridge, the seated, bound Romana is seen, from Lazlo's POV, in full length. The camera moves ever closer and Romana screams as a hairy claw bursts into the right hand side of the frame. Her scream blends into the equally chilling scream of Peter Howell's reinterpretation of the main theme as the scene cuts to the episode's end titles.

This is a recognisable televisual moment in **Doctor Who**, a cliffhanger featuring the monster threatening the companion or the Doctor, borrowing heavily from horror cinema and making a victim's scream indistinguishable from the 'sting' of the unearthly theme music[274]. However, the climax to episode 2 presupposes that Lazlo is a threat and it resembles the climactic moment in *La Belle et la Bête*, where Beauty is first prevented from leaving the castle by the Beast. Cocteau fills the screen with a close-up of Beauty gasping in shock as the Beast suddenly appears and she faints. After the Beast carries her back to her room in the castle, Cocteau presents the first proper close-up of the Beast from her POV, when his face looms into the camera as Beauty recovers, and he again frightens her. Lazlo's freeing of Romana in episode 3 restages this action. Joyce offers a momentary glimpse, from Romana's POV, of the horribly scarred Lazlo, burnt during Aldo and Royce's attempt to revive him, before revealing his true intention is to rescue her. Apparently, Pauline Cox's makeup for the Tharil's burns was too effective and, in post-production, 'Lazlo's close-up at the end of part two was shifted, using a Quantel zoom, so that not too much of his scarred appearance was in vision. It is not known on whose authority this was done.'[275]

Cocteau's influence can also be seen when Lazlo rescues the recaptured Romana in the ship's hold. They link their palms, both go

---

[274] Wood, Tat, 'Why Did the "Sting" Matter?' in *About Time #3*, p61.
[275] 'Production', *In-Vision* #50.

out of phase, instantly travel to the gateway and pass through the mirror. Joyce matches Romana's journey with a similar one, when the Doctor and the Tharil child link hands and glide through the monochrome images of the Tharil palace.

Later, in episode 4, the Doctor, Romana and Biroc press their hands together, upon Biroc's instruction to the Doctor to 'do nothing', and they fade away. As well as acknowledging the camera's slow travel through the baroque surroundings of the palace in *Marienbad*, their gliding through the monochrome garden and interiors of the Tharil palace also picks up on Beauty's arrival at the Beast's castle, running in slow motion past rows of human candelabra and gliding through corridors lined with billowing drapes. Beauty's witnessing of the curse that forces the Beast to obey animal instinct, hunt and kill lesser species (he arrives at her door, troubled and with his claws smoking from the kill) and the calming effect her presence has on this bestiality, culminates in a sequence where they promenade hand in claw through his garden bordered with stone statues of animals and she allows him to drink water cupped in her hand. This dissonance between the appearance and nature of monstrosity is retold visually and thematically in *Warriors' Gate* through the interaction between Romana and Lazlo and 'is signifying a point of tactile connection between two worlds of the story.'[276] Not only do they travel to the gateway hand in hand but, having arrived in the palace gardens, Romana also mimics Beauty's empathy with the cursed Beast when she reaches up and gently touches Lazlo's face, the burns now healed by the effects of crossing through the mirror (also combined with water from a fountain in the first draft script).

---

[276] Smart, 'Jean Cocteau and the Realm of Videographic Fantasy'.

However, the Doctor also appreciates what is in the nature of the beast, both human and Tharil. While the Doctor attends the Tharil feast, Biroc claims that 'the universe is our garden', made possible through the Tharils' mastery of the time winds. The Doctor cannily observes that even at the height of their empire they 'don't do badly for staff' but when a human servant is mistreated and he is told bluntly 'they're only people', it confirms his suspicions that the Tharils are enslavers just as callous as the humans who will eventually usurp them. 'The weak enslave themselves, Doctor, you and I know that,' pronounces Biroc. The Doctor, considering this, fills his goblet to the brim, violently upends it and snaps, 'this is no way to run an empire!' [277] This is the payoff to that subtle acknowledgment in episode 1, where the Doctor rights the fallen goblet on the table in the cobwebbed hall. He experiences a cycle of history where this concluding action becomes the story's beginning as the Tharils seek to redeem themselves from human slavery.

Cocteau's film is also a tale of masculine redemption, in the lifting of an ancient curse, and it emphasises these dual natures in the figures of the Beast and Beauty's human suitor, Avenant. Both are played by Jean Marais and through these roles Cocteau 'interrogates notions of light and dark, arrogance and humility, nobility and baseness.'[278] Not only does *Warriors' Gate* attempt to deal with what constitutes the natures of slave and master and the relation of hunter to prey, but, like *La Belle et la Bête*, it also explores aspects of 'man's bestial

---

[277] *Warriors' Gate*, episode 3.
[278] Gutierrez, Anna Katrina, *Mixed Magic: Global-Local Dialogues in Fairy Tales for Young Readers*, p185.

nature in contrast to the Beast's natural bestiality.'[279] The lion-like Tharils may be operating on animal instinct but they gain a sense of humility when humanity devises a way to penetrate the time winds and enslave them. Unlike other examples of human enslavement narratives seen in several Dalek stories, from *The Dalek Invasion of Earth* (1964) to *Evolution of the Daleks* (2007), and those of alien enslavement in *The Impossible Planet* (2006) and *Planet of the Ood* (2008), the oppositions between master and slave in *Warriors' Gate* are more ambiguous and question 'who the audience should sympathise with, who the good guys are.'[280] The Tharils may have fallen from grace but their redemption is patterned after the deaths of both Avenant and the Beast in Cocteau's film, where the conflicted nature of man and beast is transformed by Beauty's love to 'make way for Prince Ardent [...] a schema of masculinity that emerges from the synthesis of Beast and Avenant and as such presumably contains the best elements of both characters.'[281] When Romana elects to help the Tharils throw off their dubious past, she is, in effect, the embodiment of Beauty taking the hand of Prince Ardent and flying away with him into the clouds at the end of Cocteau's film.

Cocteau's *Orphée* and its sequel *Le Testament d'Orphée* further embellish the concept of travelling between different universes that Gallagher first devised in his outline for 'The Dream Time'. Both of Cocteau's films revise the Greek myth of Orpheus and Eurydice and

---

[279] Hearne, Betsy, *Beauty and the Beast: Visions and Revisions of an Old Tale*, p82.
[280] Sleight, Graham, *The Doctor's Monsters: Meanings of the Monstrous in Doctor Who*, pp141-42.
[281] Gutierrez, *Mixed Magic*, p185.

its contemplation of love, death and the afterlife. The musician Orpheus is overcome with grief when his wife Eurydice dies after being bitten by a snake. He journeys into the Underworld to bring her back and persuades Hades and Persephone to release her. Orpheus is instructed to walk ahead of Eurydice and is forbidden from looking back at her. As they leave the Underworld, he is so tormented he looks back, condemns her to death and she vanishes forever. The tragedy has been reworked in every medium, from opera, fine art and theatre, to film and television and graphic novel.

Although Cocteau retains elements of the original myth, he makes Orpheus a famous poet in post-war France. After he witnesses the death of his younger rival Cégeste, Cégeste's benefactor the Princess and her chauffeur Heurtebise take Cégeste and Orpheus to a mysterious ruined château where she reanimates Cégeste's corpse. Abandoning Orpheus, they disappear through a mirror. Heurtebise drives Orpheus home to his neglected wife Euridyce. As Heurtebise falls in love with Eurydice, Orpheus becomes obsessed with the Death-like figure of the Princess. When Eurydice is killed, Heurtebise helps Orpheus journey through the mirror into a ruined Zone, the Underworld, where he must choose between Eurydice and the Princess. A tribunal returns Eurydice to life on condition that Orpheus does not look upon her for the rest of his life. Inevitably, she suffers her mythical fate when he sees her reflection in a mirror.

David Rolinson's suggestion 'it's very *Warriors' Gate* to mirror a mirror'[282] is foreshadowed in a cryptic radio announcement, one of several that Orpheus becomes obsessed with in *Orphée*, that 'the

---

[282] Rolinson, '(Times and) Spaces of Television'.

mirrors would do well to reflect again... three times'[283], which is restated in the Gundan's aural history of the Tharils: 'there are three physical gateways. There are three, and the three are one. The whole of this domain. The ancient arch. The mirrors.'[284] As indicated previously, this mirroring reoccurs thematically throughout Gallagher's scripts and televisually in Joyce's direction. Biroc and Lazlo guiding the Doctor and Romana into their world reflect Heurtebise escorting Orpheus to the Zone. The Zone's ruined Gothic architecture, which Cocteau filmed in a bombed-out military academy, is akin to the gateway and the cobwebbed, abandoned banqueting hall. Gallagher's first draft of episode 4 also ends with the ghostly figures of Rorvik and the crew disappearing into the mirrors, on their own journey into the Underworld. Joyce attempted to replicate Cocteau's techniques from *Orphée* when Heurtebise advises Orpheus, in preparing to enter the Underworld, to wear special gloves because 'with them you will enter mirrors like water.'[285] To depict this Cocteau had Jean Marais, as Orpheus, slowly plunge his hands into a large vat of mercury. Joyce wanted to use this technique to show the Gundans and the Tharils passing through the mirror but Mat Irvine advised him that 'mercury is not allowed in studio and we would have to explore the possibility of using it under controlled conditions.'[286] For safety reasons several tests were pre-filmed and 'a Gundan axe was mounted on a rotating

---

[283] *Orphée.*

[284] *Warriors' Gate*, episode 2.

[285] *Orphée.*

[286] BBC WAC file T65/169/1. Assistant to director Joyce Stansfeld's visual effects team meeting notes, 4 August 1980.

spindle and sliced into the shiny mercury. They also tried the same effect with a Tharil hand, but neither really worked.'[287] Instead, Joyce's actors passed through a gap in green CSO drapes hung over the mirror arches. A locked-off camera was pointed at another mirror reflecting the banqueting hall and Robin Lobb lined this up with the CSO shot, combining it with an electronic shimmer effect to complete the illusion.

Cocteau's scenes of Heurtebise returning Orpheus through the Zone and back to the other side of the mirror, by reversing the footage of their original journey to the point when Orpheus donned the gloves, is suggestive of the timeslip that occurs in episode 3 of *Warriors' Gate*. Joyce also uses the idea of the camera looking back through the mirror, where Cocteau shows the Princess and her henchmen stepping through it toward the camera, which represents the audience's POV. Gallagher described similar camera positions in his scripts, in the sequence in episode 3 where the Doctor, on the other side of the mirror, first meets Biroc. Again, Joyce's deep-space staging, with Rorvik's party out of focus in the banqueting hall behind the Doctor and Biroc, adds a three-dimensional quality to the imagery. In episode 4, when the Doctor is ordered at gunpoint by Rorvik to reveal the secret of the mirrors, echoing Heurtebise's reveal of 'the secret of secrets'[288] that will allow Orpheus to enter the mirrors in *Orphée*, he speaks to Biroc through the mirror and a sound effect is added to suggest that the mirror is between them. A series of descending notes, presumably added by composer Peter Howell, also acts as a score or sound effect when each person enters

---

[287] Wiggins, *Warriors' Gate* DVD production text, episode 2.
[288] *Orphée.*

the mirrors, and is the equivalent of the tuning fork sound motif that Cocteau uses as his characters pass through the mirrors. The idea of having the Doctor with his back to Rorvik's party as he speaks to Biroc, who also has his back to the Doctor, is perhaps analogous to how, in *Orphée*, Orpheus must never see Eurydice, so they converse with each other, but not face to face.

Cocteau's notion that the fluctuating dreamlike space of the Zone represents 'the margin of life, a no-man's land between life and death, where one is neither fully dead nor fully alive'[289], is replicated in the slowly collapsing void of *Warriors' Gate*. It also underscores the themes of Baker's final season, with the Doctor's prolonged postponement of death manifested in the form of the Watcher in *Logopolis*, and where 'the delaying of death is vital', interlinked as it is with the fight against entropy and decay[290]. The Tharils' conquest of time and space is described to the Doctor by the Gundans in similar terms: 'the masters created an empire, draining the life of the ordinary world'[291] and sapped the life from N-Space before the tables were turned by their former slaves.

The cycle of history in *Warriors' Gate*, a disorder and order that has seemingly taken its toll on the universe, is representative of the lingering death that, through the power of mathematics, the Logopolitans are holding in abeyance with their CVEs that drain away this excess entropy in *Logopolis*. The ruins of the Gothic gateway

---

[289] Cocteau's notes to the film quoted in Williams, *Jean Cocteau* p126.
[290] Rolinson, '(Times and) Spaces of Television'.
[291] *Warriors' Gate*, episode 2.

replicate the Zone in *Orphée*, which is described by Heurtebise as 'made of the memories of men and the ruins of their habits.'[292] For Cocteau it may have been an allegory of the German Occupation of France, of the country's potential redemption from ambiguous collaborations and violent relationships. *Orphée* and, particularly, *Le Testament d'Orphée* explore his own redemption as an artist through 'Proustian journeys up and down the corridors of time'[293].

Le Testament d'Orphée is full of moments concerned with 'the relativity and reversibility of time and its connection with space, resurrection and metamorphosis, ageing and the passage between life and death.'[294] A documentary incorporating reportage and myth, it depicts Cocteau's own death and resurrection, symbolised in a brief sequence where a pool of blood and a discarded hibiscus flower burst into bright red colour against a black-and-white background. Cocteau's personal history, discarded in monochrome but then resurrected in colour, is traced onto the dreamlike colour figures keyed into the frozen black-and-white palace and gardens in *Warriors' Gate*.

---

[292] *Orphée*.
[293] Williams, *Jean Cocteau*, p129.
[294] Williams, *Jean Cocteau*, p93.

CHAPTER 8: 'THE INDIVIDUAL CONFRONTED BY THE DESOLATE UNIVERSE'

At the visual effects team meeting on 4 August 1980, the depiction of both the gateway and the rooms coming off the banqueting hall was envisaged as a combination of the exterior and interior sets built in the studio, and extensions painted on glass mounted in front of the camera. However, Joyce strove for a more poetic ambience and took the unusual course of commissioning freelance landscape painter David H Smith to produce a conceptual painting. This kind of conceptual artwork was commonly undertaken at the BBC by the various departments working on **Doctor Who**. Smith devised perhaps one of the most significant visual symbols in *Warriors' Gate* – the ruined three-windowed Gothic arch and crumbling entrance of the gateway.

His final design helped Story and Irvine plan and coordinate their efforts, with Story able to determine how much of the gateway entrance he needed to build as a set in studio to match what Irvine would realise as models. For the studio, the full scale lower entrance was sculpted out of jabolite and for the model filming three plaster miniatures were taken from moulds based on clay sculptures. Two four-foot versions were used in the explosive finale to episode 4 and a smaller version was used in perspective shots alongside the TARDIS and privateer models. Despite pressure from Nathan-Turner to shoot the model effects on video[295], the effects team demanded that the destruction of the privateer and gateway models 'must be on

---

[295] Wiggins, *Warriors' Gate* DVD production text, episode 4.

film.'[296] Shot twice at high speed on 35mm and 16mm to achieve the required slow motion, Irvine provided 'four pieces of film, all taken from different angles. I did not edit and cut the film together. Paul did that job, although I must say he made it a much longer and more spectacular scene than I was anticipating.'[297]

Joyce's commissioning of Smith's concept art also showed he was determined from the outset to use a wide set of references to create the poetic, philosophical nature of *Warriors' Gate*. The art's resemblance to the work of German Romantic painter Caspar David Friedrich (1774-1840), particularly *Monastery Graveyard in the Snow* (c1817-19), was no coincidence. For Joyce, *Warriors' Gate* posed:

> '...an existential question, and David and I discussed that and we were both fans of Friedrich's anyway. And that sort of quest... a journey... an alien landscape. There's so many things that made it perfect and then, the crumbling gate, you know. I mean, [...] it wasn't a deliberate homage to *Planet of the Apes* [1968] but, in a sense, it's the hand coming out of the sand. It's a bit like that.'[298]

Friedrich's work and the German Romantic movement of artists, musicians, poets and philosphers that formed around 1800, embraced a number of attitudes and concerns:

> '...a heightened sensitivity to the natural world, combined with a belief in nature's correspondence to the mind; a

[296] BBC WAC file T65/169/1. Visual effects team meeting notes, 4 August 1980.
[297] Irvine, 'Cause an Effect'.
[298] Joyce, interview with author.

passion for the equivocal, the indeterminate, the obscure and the faraway (objects shrouded in fog, a distant fire in the darkness, mountains merging with clouds, etc.); a celebration of subjectivity bordering on solipsism, often coupled with a morbid desire that that self be lost in nature's various infinities; an infatuation with death; valorisation of night over day, emblematising a reaction against Enlightenment and rationalism; a nebulous but all-pervading mysticism; and a melancholy, sentimental longing or nostalgia which can border on kitsch.'[299]

The movement's search for meaning in an increasingly secular age was a reaction to Enlightenment philosophers and scientists who challenged the orthodoxies of religion and monarchy with reason, scientific reductionism and rationalism. Some of that antagonism can be found in *Warriors' Gate*, and it is ironic that a theoretical physicist like David Bohm was, at the time of the story's broadcast, questioning the dominant interpretation of quantum mechanics by proposing that complete scientific clarity about the quantum universe was not possible. His theory of the implicate order, which his peers believed was perilously close to a non-rational anti-Enlightenment philosophy, asked scientists to question their basic assumptions about nature and 'move beyond mechanistic and even mathematical paradigms.'[300] He believed science, religion and art would merge and that perhaps scientists could gain new modes of perception and access to deeper levels of consciousness through an

---

[299] Koerner, Joseph Leo, *Caspar David Friedrich and the Subject of Landscape*, p29.
[300] Horgan, John, 'David Bohm, Quantum Mechanics and Enlightenment'.

understanding of artistic creation or Eastern religions and philosophies.

The indeterminate nature of the gateway is expressed in Gallagher's first draft description:

> 'Two massive wooden doors set in an arch of mason-cut rock, two decayed pillars supporting a partly-collapsed lintel, a ruined statue to one side, an empty plinth with a heap of rubble around it on the other. One of the doors is slightly ajar. The rocks are white and grey, and they blend off into the surroundings imperceptibly.'[301]

Gallagher's concept of the featureless, enveloping white void and the shifting sense of space and distance in *Warriors' Gate*, perhaps similar to the white void which presages the TARDIS's entry into the Land of Fiction in *The Mind Robber* (1968), matches the sensibility of Friedrich's painting *The Monk by the Sea* (painted 1808-10). Depicting a tiny, lone figure in a monk's habit marooned on a beach against a brooding dark sea and oppressive sky, Friedrich's allegorical use of nature suggests 'the individual confronted by the desolate universe' where 'infinity becomes the true subject of the painting' and is remarkable, according to a Berlin newspaper, for its 'apocalyptic featurelessness.'[302]

Gallagher first describes the void via a perspective through the TARDIS doors as Biroc arrives in episode 1: 'It is brilliant white, and

---

[301] Hull Archives. Gallagher, 'The Dream Time', episode 1, p32.
[302] Wolf, Norbert, *Caspar David Friedrich 1774-1840: The Painter of Stillness*, pp31-35.

featureless – except that, in the distance, there is a figure running towards the angled aperture.'[303] Various descriptions of small, silhouetted figures appearing in white or blank mists pepper the original scripts. He also suggests its vastness with the stage direction 'out in the void, with the TARDIS small in the distance which is exaggerated by the use of a wide angle on the lens.'[304] Friedrich saw the overwhelming power of nature and the universe as a religious experience and attempted to render this on canvas, using symbols and motifs about life, death and the impermanence of humanity. His landscapes increasingly featured ruined monasteries or churches, single figures or groups in silhouette that were often small in scale in comparison to the vastness of nature, and religious iconography and symbols of mortality such as crucifixes, gravestones and coffins. Like the topography of *Warriors' Gate*, 'Friedrich's paintings seem to represent a familiar nowhere; various places, moments and impressions are combined into images that appear both real and constructed, familiar and disorienting'[305]and conjure up themes of entropy and decay. He is distinguished by 'the elements of a "negative beauty" – deliberate monotony, formal repetition, the unmistakable sound of emptiness within the orchestral whole of the picture, and the strange coupling of proximity to nature and distance from nature.'[306]

Gallagher's scripts and their later revisions depict dramatically shifting distances and scales when the blank void's collapse is made tangible as journeys between recognisable landmarks – the TARDIS,

---

[303] Hull Archives. Gallagher, 'The Dream Time', episode 1, p10.
[304] Hull Archives. Gallagher, 'The Dream Time', episode 1, p36.
[305] Whittington, Karl, 'Caspar David Friedrich's Medieval Burials'.
[306] Wolf, *Caspar David Friedrich*, p34.

the gateway and the privateer – contract. A closer comparison of the gateway's design with Friedrich's *Monastery Graveyard in the Snow* yields much more than an homage to its Gothic architecture or a sense of the apocalyptic. Sadly, the original painting no longer exists as it was destroyed during air-raids on Berlin in the Second World War. That only black-and-white photographs of it exist is ironic, given that this remnant of Friedrich's landscape finds some equivalence with Joyce's photographs of Powis Castle used to represent the monochrome Tharil palace and gardens. The centre of Friedrich's painting is dominated by three immense Gothic arched windows coupled with the ruined entrance to a monastery, and it's clearly the inspiration for Smith's concept art. The ruins are surrounded by the familiar motifs of gnarled old trees reaching into the sky, a snowy forest floor scattered with tombstones and, weaving through them, a procession of monks escorting a coffin.

Just as Joyce and Smith reproduced its central architectural elements for the gateway, Friedrich's painting is itself a collage of his previous work, with the leafless trees lifted from *Dolmen in the Snow* (1807) and *The Abbey in the Oak Wood* (1809-10) and the small ruin reproduced from his early drawings. Friedrich's works are constructed from various sources, just as the transmitted version of *Warriors' Gate* is constructed from the diverse influences and ideas informing Gallagher's scripts and Joyce's direction. Equally, the painting provides a thematic correspondence to it and the central ideas in season 18. Themes of death and resurrection pervade the painting, with the passage of the coffin into decaying ruins that have melded with the trees articulating 'the return to nature through death to show interconnectedness and wholeness, rather than fragmentation or loss.' Friedrich translated his relationship with nature into a melancholic meditation on death and many historians have associated his works 'with the transcendence of death through religious experience in nature.'[307]

In *Warriors' Gate*, the characters are positioned between a deterministic, rational universe, symbolised by the privateer and its slavish dependence on technology, and one where the dogma of cruel but dead empires, symbolised in the ruins and the decaying banqueting hall, are transcended by a moral and spiritual rebirth in a building that closely resembles a church. Like Cocteau in *Le Testament d'Orphée* or the time-sensitive Tharils, Friedrich visualises and predicts his own death and transcendence in the images of monks carrying the coffin into the ruins of the monastery. In the climax to *Warriors' Gate*, a Quantel effect replicates Friedrich's motif and shows a procession of out-of-phase Tharils walking away from the wreckage of the privateer and into the remains of the gateway. For the Tharils, the past is dead and they will soon have a Time Lord to guide them into the future. This melancholic tone is later epitomised in *Logopolis*, with its own procession of Logopolitan monks and the distant figure of the Watcher.

Just as *Warriors' Gate* connects the viewer to the idea of an unfettered visualisation of the universe, one freed of rigid assumptions, Friedrich's work connects the viewer to his gaze. He advises in his notes on aesthetics, 'close your bodily eye, so that you may see your picture first with the spiritual eye. Then bring what you saw in the dark into the light, so that it may have an effect on others, shining inwards from outside.'[308] Like Bohm's entreaty to visualise

---

[307] Whittington, 'Caspar David Friedrich's Medieval Burials'.
[308] Grave, Johannes, *Caspar David Friedrich*, p203.

the deeper level of reality, many of Friedrich's paintings incorporate a double gaze by placing figures in the centre foreground of the canvas. It's best seen in two works from 1818, *The Wanderer Above the Sea of Fog* and *Woman Before the Rising Sun (Woman Before the Setting Sun)*, where the central axis of the paintings is occupied by a figure, known as the *Rückenfigur*, with their back to the viewer. The viewer of these works is sublimated into the role of the painted figure. These paintings also describe how those landscapes are being observed by the figures in the painting. The subject becomes the act of seeing a landscape and the hidden reality of the variables and conditions that affect the view. The observer standing behind the painted figure, who is unable to turn around and look back, suggests the Orpheus myth that Cocteau reinterpreted in *Orphée* and that informed the foregrounding of figures and objects in Gallagher's scripts and Joyce's camera shots.

Further thematic connections with Friedrich emerge from Samuel Beckett's visit to Germany in 1937. There he saw Friedrich's *Two Men Contemplating the Moon* (1819-20) and its composition, placing two still figures in front of a landscape with the dominating images of a tree and the moon, inspired the opening scene of *Waiting for Godot*. This establishes a line of fateful character duos, from the pair in Friedrich's painting, to those in Beckett and Stoppard, and to Aldo and Royce in *Warriors' Gate*. Finally, in Friedrich's motif of figures looking longingly out into vast, overwhelming landscapes 'he empties his canvas in order to imagine, through an invocation of the void, an infinite unrepresentable God.'[309] This resonates with Joyce's

---

[309] Koerner, *Caspar David Friedrich and the Subject of Landscape*, p22.

aspirations for *Warriors' Gate* to depict humanity searching for meaning in an unknowable universe:

> 'Do you recall the closing sequences of *2001: A Space Odyssey*? The attempted replica by advanced beings of a French château or similar interior? To make the earthling feel at home. Maybe in some respects the same could be true of the gateway. In other words it does not mark in any sense an actual location, or form part of a real landscape; rather it is a simulacrum placed by unknown hands as a marker for future travellers to recognise as an entrance into a world they might in some way recognise and beyond that, come to understand.'[310]

Again, this matches certain elements of *Warriors' Gate*, with astronaut Bowman's journey through the Star Gate in Kubrick's film. Bowman's death and transfiguration into the Star Child takes place in an ornate Louis XIV room. Its rococo embellishments resemble the interiors of the palace at Marienbad and the black-and-white images of the long gallery of Powis Castle. Bowman's room is perhaps a representation, plucked from his mind by the unseen, god-like alien intelligences, of humankind's cultural achievements, but Kubrick renders it, through the intense underfloor white lighting, as an echoing, sterile chamber or void. Most significantly, timeslips occur as Bowman gradually ages and moves from his space pod, dines alone, and journeys to his death and resurrection. He observes these as a *Rückenfigur*, in a chain of short scenes where he sees his older self in the topography of the room, then becomes that self who in turns observes the next stage in his evolution. In one scene, he

---

[310] Joyce, email to author, 4 August 2018.

174

knocks a glass onto the floor and as he stretches to pick up the pieces he glances to the bedroom and sees another older self, bedridden and close to death. Perhaps this sequence was an influence on the timeslip, symbolised in the overturned goblet, between the banqueting halls of past and present in *Warriors' Gate* and symbolic of Biroc and the Tharils eventually out-evolving their captors.

In Kubrick's film, it is an encounter with an alien culture that influences humanity to rise above its animalistic and barbarous past, whereas in *Warriors' Gate* the humans and the Tharils are mirror images of this cycle, reflections of the human beast and the noble animal. Gallagher recalled that, although unintentional, connections were made with Kubrick's film: 'A Canadian guy recently buttonholed me at a convention and said, "My God! You're the man who wrote *Warriors' Gate*. That story is the *2001* of **Doctor Who**!" Ah, well, steady on!'[311]

---

[311] Cook, 'In Space No-one Can Hear You Scream'.

CONCLUSION

Warriors' Gate's reputation stems from Joyce and Gallagher's atypical approach to storytelling. Its realisation challenged prevailing BBC studio practices and the accepted hierarchies between director, producer, writer and script editor. Joyce's direction was, in a rare instance, affiliated to his co-writing of the final *Warriors' Gate* scripts. Having imprinted upon them his personality, influences and preferences as a writer and director, it is reasonable to say he was more privileged than most as one author of the transmitted episodes. However, Stephen Gallagher's first draft scripts were the predominant origin of the characters, the story and many of the ideas, references and concepts realised in the transmitted version of *Warriors' Gate*. BBC Audio's restored novelisation of those drafts offers an alternative, but equally valid, version of his story.

This authorship was an iteration of a more complex and contested set of relationships. **Doctor Who** continues to be an auteur enterprise because its format is reconfigured by the specific authorial remit of each of its producers. Therefore, *Warriors' Gate* also represents a body of work made by Nathan-Turner, its modernising producer, and the overall narrative that Bidmead, its script editor, created for season 18.

Despite the changes in television production since the making of *Warriors' Gate*, authorship has largely remained the privilege of the producers of **Doctor Who**. Since its revival, Russell T Davies, Steven Moffat and Chris Chibnall have, as showrunners (executive producers and head writers) controlled its authorial intent. This echoes developments in US television, where this privilege became absorbed into the role of the showrunner, with Joss Whedon and

David Chase, for example, becoming influential as television producer-writer-director auteurs.

Gallagher went on to control his own authorship by forging a television career in Britain and the US. Having written for, developed, supervised, and executive produced several television shows, he compared his US experiences to those on British productions:

> '...all the writers had producer credits, individual writers produced their own episodes within a show, they were on set during shooting and if the director needed to make changes they [...] asked the writer if that was OK and what the change might be. All the writers together participated in the shaping of the show and the showrunner had the last word over all creative elements. That doesn't happen in Britain. What happens [...] is you deliver your script and then you watch as others do their thing with it.'[312]

Davies, Moffat and Chibnall have produced episodes they have written or co-written but other writers on **Doctor Who** have not always been afforded that privilege. To ensure scripts were good enough for production, Davies acknowledged he upset some writers by rewriting their scripts: 'I write the final draft of almost all scripts - and that draft becomes the shooting script. I might change at least 30%, often 60% and sometimes almost 100%.'[313]

---

[312] **Toby Hadoke's Who's Round** #166.
[313] Davies, Russell T, and Benjamin Cook, *The Writer's Tale: The Final Chapter*, p150.

Neil Gaiman recently related his experience of writing *Nightmare in Silver* (2013) for the series. Like Gallagher, he was aggrieved that he was unable to improve the script by 'having a say in what actually got to the screen, a say in what got changed, a say in what got rewritten, a say in the colour scheme, a say in all those things.'[314] As a result of his experience, he became the showrunner of Amazon's adaptation of **Good Omens** (2019), a novel he wrote with his late friend Terry Pratchett, to guide its onscreen realisation.

The convergence of the television and film industries continues to redefine these hierarchies and the cinematic stylings of television drama. Netflix, HBO and Showtime have invited well-known film directors to write, produce and direct their own television projects. Recently, director David Lynch's 18-hour **Twin Peaks: The Return** (2017), a television sequel just as unorthodox an example of Lynch's signature cinematic canon as any of his other works, reopened the debate about the increasingly narrow distinction between film and television. However, in British television the television auteur is perhaps more the privilege of someone like Sally Wainwright, who recently created, wrote, produced, cast and directed the crime drama **Happy Valley** (2014-). Does Wainwright, in a medium that privileges the producer-writer, have a televisual style as a director?

A television director's style is increasingly defined today by new technology, the industry's economics and practices, and the aesthetics prescribed by executive producers who, in all likelihood, direct and write shows too. Paul Joyce believes that the power still 'remains firmly with the writer and producer who, nowadays, is

---

[314] Quoted in 'Neil Gaiman: "My **Doctor Who** experience left me with a bad taste in my mouth".'

more often actually the writer/producer.' He questions whether a director's style can survive the imperatives driving successful contemporary drama series:

> '...And we have great ones tumbling over each other: **Life on Mars** [2006-7], **Spooks** [2002-11], **Luther** [2010-], the list grows daily or monthly. But where in all this output is the director's stamp?'[315]

Renowned British film director Ben Wheatley directed two episodes of **Doctor Who** (*Deep Breath* and *Into the Dalek*) in 2014, and his visual flourishes and casting choices can be detected within the programme's established production and narrative ethos. It may be possible, given further in-depth analysis, to interpret the specific styles of auteur producer-writer-directors Euros Lyn, James Hawes, James Strong, Douglas Mackinnon, Nick Hurran and Rachel Talalay, all of whom have directed many episodes, in relation to the narrative complexity of their stories.

It would also be valuable to interrogate the television style of Graeme Harper, who directed episodes of the original series and its revival. An analysis of Harper's distinctive work on *The Caves of Androzani* and *Revelation of the Daleks*, comparing it with his recent work on the series, might show how changes in the industry have altered his personal style, including his use of cameras, space and lighting, editing and shooting styles and their relevance to other film and television genres and, importantly, to the development of narrative complexity in **Doctor Who**.

---

[315] Joyce, email to author, 21 December 2018.

BIBLIOGRAPHY

Documents

BBC Written Archives Centre.

>**Doctor Who** Serial 5S, *Warriors' Gate*, T65/169/1.

>**Doctor Who** Serial 5S, *Warriors' Gate*, T65/256/1.

>**Doctor Who**, *Warriors' Gate* (camera scripts).

>**The Other Side** *Solid Geometry*, T62/6/1.

>**Play For Today** *Keep Smiling*, Audience Research Reports 18 March 1980, R9/7/163.

>Television *Weekly* Programme Review meetings 16 January 1980, 14 and 21 January 1981.

BBC copyright content reproduced courtesy of the British Broadcasting Corporation. All rights reserved.

University of Hull Archives at the Hull History Centre.

>UDGA *Warriors' Gate* files 1 and 2.

>UDGA **The Last Rose of Summer**, **Hunters' Moon** and **The Babylon Run** files.

>UDGA *An Alternative to Suicide* file.

>UDGA General Correspondence files 2 and 3.

Doctor Who, *Warriors' Gate* (rehearsal scripts). Private collection.

Doctor Who, *Warriors' Gate*. BBC Audio manuscript assembly and first edit, May 2018. Courtesy of Stephen Gallagher.

Books

Andrews, Hannah, *Television and British Cinema: Convergence and Divergence Since 1990*. Basingstoke and New York, Palgrave Macmillan, 2014, ISBN 9781137311160.

Baker, Brian, *Science Fiction: A Reader's Guide to Essential Criticism*. London, Palgrave, 2014. ISBN 9780230228146.

Bates, Julie, *Beckett's Art of Salvage: Writing and Material Imagination, 1932-1987*. Cambridge, Cambridge University Press, 2017. ISBN 9781107167049.

Beckett, Samuel, *The Complete Dramatic Works*. 1986. London, Faber and Faber, 2006. ISBN 9780571229154.

Bester, Alfred, *The Demolished Man*. 1953. London, Gollancz, 2004. ISBN 1857988221.

Bignell, Jonathan, and Stephen Lacey, eds, *British Television Drama: Past, Present and Future*. 2000. Basingstoke and New York, Palgrave Macmillan, 2014. ISBN 9781137327574.

Bignell, Jonathan and Stephen Lacey, 'Introduction'.

Bignell, Jonathan and Stephen Lacey, eds, *Popular Television Drama: Critical Perspectives*. Manchester and New York, Manchester University Press, 2005. ISBN 9780719069338.

Bignell, Jonathan, ''Space for "Quality": Negotiating with the Daleks'.

Bohm, David, *Wholeness and the Implicate Order*. 1980. London and New York, Routledge, 2002. ISBN 9780415289795.

Booy, Miles, *Love and Monsters: The Doctor Who Experience, 1979 to the Present*. London and New York, IB Tauris and Co Ltd, 2012. ISBN 9781848854796.

Burk, Graeme, and Robert Smith?, *Who's 50: The 50 Doctor Who Stories to Watch Before You Die – An Unofficial Companion*. Toronto, ECW Press, 2013. ISBN 9781770411661.

Butler, David, ed, *Time and Relative Dissertations in Space: Critical Perspectives on Doctor Who*. Manchester, Manchester University Press, 2007. ISBN 9780719076824.

> Rolinson, Dave, '"**Who** Done It": Discourses of Authorship in the John Nathan-Turner Era'.

> Hills, Matt, 'Televisuality without Television? The Big Finish Audios and Discourses of 'tele-centric' **Doctor Who**'.

Caldwell, John Thornton, *Televisuality: Style, Crisis and Authority in American Television*. New Brunswick and New Jersey, Rutgers University Press, 1994. ISBN 9780813521640.

Capra, Fritjof, *The Tao of Physics: An Exploration of the Parallels Between Modern Physics and Eastern Mysticism*. 1976. London, Flamingo, 1982. ISBN 9780006544890.

Cocteau, Jean, *Beauty and the Beast: Scenario and Dialogs*. Robert M Hammond, ed, New York, New York University Press, 1970. ISBN 9780814733578.

Cooke, Lez, *British Television Drama: A History*. London, British Film Institute, 2003. ISBN 9780851708850.

Cooke, Lez, *A Sense of Place: Regional British Television Drama, 1956-82*. Manchester, Manchester University Press, 2012. ISBN 9780719086786.

Couper, Stephen, *Dying of Paradise*. Glasgow, Sphere Books Ltd, 1982. ISBN 9780722137956.

Davies, Russell T, and Benjamin Cook, *The Writer's Tale: The Final Chapter*. London, BBC Books, 2016. ISBN 9781846078613.

Demastes, William, *The Cambridge Introduction to Tom Stoppard*. New York, Cambridge University Press, 2012. ISBN 9781107606128.

Devereux, Eoin, Aileen Dillane and Martin Power, eds, *David Bowie: Critical Perspectives*. New York and Oxon, Routledge, 2015. ISBN 9780415745727.

> Eoin Devereux, Aileen Dillane and Martin Power, 'Culminating Sounds and (En)Visions - *Ashes to Ashes* and the Case for Pierrot'.

Dick, Philip K, *The Man in the High Castle*. 1962. London, Penguin Books, 2001. ISBN 9780141186672.

Dick, Philip K, *The Minority Report and Other Classic Stories*. 1956. New York, Citadel Press, 2016. ISBN 9780806537955.

Dick, Philip K, *The Simulacra*. 1964. London, Gollancz, 2004. ISBN 9780575074606.

Dick, Philip K, *The Three Stigmata of Palmer Eldritch*. 1964. London, Gollancz, 2004. ISBN 9780575074804.

Dick, Philip K, *The World Jones Made*. 1956. London, Gollancz, 2003. ISBN 9780575074576.

Edwards, William Howell, *An Introduction to Aboriginal Societies*. 1998. South Melbourne, Victoria, Thomson Social Science Press, 2007. ISBN 9780170177603.

Gallagher, Stephen, *Chimera*. London, Sphere Books Ltd, 1982. ISBN 9780722137574.

Gallagher, Steve, *The Last Rose of Summer*. London, Corgi Books Ltd, 1978. ISBN 9780552109383.

Grave, Johannes, *Caspar David Friedrich*. 2012. Munich, London and New York, Prestel Verlag, 2017. ISBN 9783791383576.

Gutierrez, Anna Katrina, *Mixed Magic: Global-Local Dialogues in Fairy Tales for Young Readers*. Amsterdam and Philadelphia, John Benjamins Publishing Company, 2017. ISBN 9789027201621.

Haldeman, Joe, *The Forever War*. 1974. London, Gollancz, 2004. ISBN 1857988086.

Haggard, H Rider, *She: A History of Adventure*. 1887. Oxford and New York, Oxford University Press, 2008. ISBN 9780199536429.

Harrison, Harry, *Bill, the Galactic Hero*. 1965. London, Gollancz, 2015. ISBN 9781473205314.

Hearne, Betsy, *Beauty and the Beast: Visions and Revisions of an Old Tale*. Chicago and London, University of Chicago Press, 1989. ISBN 9780226322391.

Hinde, Thomas, *The Day the Call Came*. 1964. London, Corgi Books Ltd, 1966.

Hofstadter, Douglas, *Gödel, Escher, Bach: An Eternal Golden Braid*. 1979. London, Penguin Books, 2000. ISBN 9780140289206.

Howe, David J, and Stephen James Walker, *Doctor Who: The Television Companion*. London, BBC Books, 1998. ISBN 9780563405887.

Hudson, June, and Piers Britton, *Refashioning the Doctor – A 'Make-over' for a Sci-Fi Icon: Costume Design Drawings by June Hudson*. California, University of Redlands, Department of Art, 2006.

Hughes, William, David Punter and Andrew Smith, eds, *The Encyclopedia of the Gothic*. Chichester, John Wiley & Sons Ltd, 2016. ISBN 9781119064602.

      Smith, Andrew, 'Degeneration'.

Independent Broadcasting Authority (IBA), *Annual Reports and Accounts 1977-78*. London, IBA, 1978. ISBN 9780900485336.

Jacobs, Jason, *The Intimate Screen: Early British Television Drama*. Oxford, Clarendon Press, 2000. ISBN 9780198742340.

Jones, Steven Swann, *The Fairy Tale: The Magic Mirror of the Imagination*. London and New York, Routledge, 2002. ISBN 9780415938914.

Kelly, Richard, ed, *Alan Clarke*. London, Faber and Faber, 1998. ISBN 9780571196098.

Koerner, Joseph Leo, *Caspar David Friedrich and the Subject of Landscape*. 1990. Second ed, London, Reaktion Books Ltd, 2009. ISBN 9781861894397.

Kooijman, Jaap, *Fabricating the Absolute Fake: America in Contemporary Pop Culture*. Amsterdam, Amsterdam University Press, 2008. ISBN 9789053564929.

Luckhurst, Roger, *Science Fiction*. Cambridge, Polity Press, 2005. ISBN 9780745628936.

Lydecker, John, *Doctor Who and Warriors' Gate*. **The Target Doctor Who Library** #71. London, WH Allen, 1982. ISBN 9780426201465.

Marson, Richard, *JN-T: The Life and Scandalous Times of John Nathan-Turner*. Surrey, Miwk Publishing Ltd, 2013. ISBN 9781908630131.

Miles, Lawrence, and Tat Wood, *1980-84: Seasons 18 to 21*. **About Time: The Unauthorised Guide to Doctor Who** #5. Illinois, Mad Norwegian Press, 2005. ISBN 9780975944646.

Miller, Jonathan, and Ian Greaves, ed, *One Thing and Another: Selected Writings 1954–2016*. London, Oberon Books Ltd, 2017. ISBN 9781783197453.

> Pasternak Slater, Ann, 'Directing Shakespeare'. Miller interview, *Quarto*, September 1980.

Mulvey, Laura, and Jamie Sexton, eds, *Experimental British Television*. Manchester and New York, Manchester University Press, 2007. ISBN 9780719075544.

> Cooke, Lez, 'An Experiment in Television Drama: John McGrath's *The Adventures of Frank*'.

Murch, Walter, *In the Blink of an Eye: A Perspective on Film Editing*. 1995. Los Angeles, Silman-James Press, 2001. ISBN 9781879505629.

Nichol, Lee, ed, *David Bohm On Creativity*. 1996. Oxon and New York, Routledge, 2004. ISBN 9780415336406.

> Wijers, Louwrien, 'Art, Dialogue, and the Implicate Order'.

Pegg, Nicholas, *The Complete David Bowie*. 2000. London, Titan Books, 2016. ISBN 9781785653650.

Rigelsford, Adrian, *Classic Who: The Harper Classics – The Making of The Caves of Androzani and Revelation of the Daleks*. London and Basingstoke, Boxtree, 1996. ISBN 9780752201887.

Rimmer, Dave, *New Romantics: The Look*. 2003. London, Omnibus Press, 2013. ISBN 9781783053117.

Shakespeare, William, *Hamlet*. 1623. Harold Jenkins, ed, London and New York, Methuen & Co Ltd, 1984. ISBN 9780416179200.

Shakespeare, William, *The Tempest*. 1623. Frank Kermode, ed, London and New York, Routledge, Chapman and Hall, 1989. ISBN 9780415027045.

Sleight, Graham, *The Doctor's Monsters: Meanings of the Monstrous in Doctor Who*. London, IB Tauris & Co Ltd, 2012. ISBN 9781848851788.

Smith, Paul, *The Classic Doctor Who DVD Compendium*. Wonderful Books, 2014. ISBN 9780957606210.

Stoppard, Tom, *Plays 5: Arcadia, The Real Thing, Night & Day, Indian Ink, Hapgood*. London, Faber and Faber, 1999. ISBN 9780571197514.

Stoppard, Tom, *Rosencrantz and Guildenstern Are Dead*. 1967. London, Faber and Faber, 2000. ISBN 9780571081820.

Talbot, Michael, *The Holographic Universe*. 1991. London, HarperCollins Publishers, 1996. ISBN 9780586091715.

Toon, John, *Full Circle*. **The Black Archive** #15. Edinburgh, Obverse Books, 2018. ISBN 9781909031630.

Tulloch, John, and Manuel Alvarado, *Doctor Who: The Unfolding Text*. London and Basingstoke, The Macmillan Press, 1983. ISBN 9780333348482.

Wilhelm, Richard, trans, *I Ching or Book of Changes*. 1951. Third ed, London, Penguin Books, 2003. ISBN 9780140192070.

Williams, James S, *French Film Directors: Jean Cocteau*. Manchester and New York, Manchester University Press, 2009. ISBN 9780719058844.

Wilson, Emma, *French Film Directors: Alain Resnais*. Manchester and New York, Manchester University Press, 2006. ISBN 9780719064074.

Wood, Tat, and Lawrence Miles, *1970-74: Seasons 7 to 11.* **About Time: The Unauthorised Guide to Doctor Who** #3. Illinois, Mad Norwegian Press, 2009. ISBN 97809975944677.

Wolf, Norbert, *Caspar David Friedrich 1774-1840: The Painter of Stillness*. 2003. Cologne, Taschen GmbH, 2018. ISBN 9783836560719.

Wollen, Peter, *Signs and Meaning in the Cinema*. 1969. Fifth ed, Basingstoke and New York, Palgrave Macmillan, 2013. ISBN 9780253181411.

Periodicals

Doctor Who: The Complete History

> Volume 32: *The Leisure Hive, Meglos*, and *Full Circle*, 22 March 2017.

> Volume 33: *State of Decay, Warriors' Gate, The Keeper of Traken* and *Logopolis*, 1 November 2017.

Doctor Who Magazine (DWM). Marvel UK, Panini, BBC, 1979-.

Arnopp, Jason, 'Science Friction'. DWM #407, cover date April 2009.

Cook, Benjamin, 'In Space No-one Can Hear You Scream'. DWM #295, cover date September 2000.

Griffiths, Peter, 'Fifth Man In'. DWM #258, cover date November 1997.

Hearn, Marcus, 'Directing Who: Lovett Bickford'. DWM #191, cover date September 1992.

MacDonald, Philip, 'Change and Decay'. DWM #185, cover date April 1992.

Morris, Jonathan, 'The Fact of Fiction: *Warriors' Gate*'. DWM #499, cover date June 2016.

Nathan-Turner, John, 'The John Nathan-Turner Memoirs Part One: It's Not Where You Start...'. DWM #233, cover date December 1995.

Spilsbury, Tom, 'The Guv'nor'. DWM #380, cover date March 2007.

Travers, Paul, 'Valley of Who'. DWM #139, cover date August 1988.

In-Vision: The Making of a Television Drama Series. Cybermark Services, 1988-2003.

Anghelides, Peter, 'Signed, Sealed, Delivered, Discarded'. Season 18 overview. #54, November 1994.

Freeman, John, 'The Man in the Control Seat', *Warriors' Gate*. #50, April 1994.

Gallagher, Stephen, 'Scripting *Warriors' Gate*: So what actually happened?' #54, November 1994.

Irvine, Mat, 'Cause an Effect', #50, April 1994.

Newman, Philip, 'Joyce Words', #50, April 1994.

'Production', *The Leisure Hive*. #46, September 1993.

'Production', #50, April 1994.

Duncan, Joseph E, 'Godot Comes: Rosencrantz and Guildenstern Are Dead'. *Ariel: A Review of International English Literature* Vol 12, No. 4 (October 1981).

Panos, Leah, 'Stylised Worlds: Colour Separation Overlay in BBC Television Plays of the 1970s'. *Critical Studies in Television* Vol 8, No. 3 (Autumn 2013).

Zohar, Danah, 'How the universe hangs together'. *The Sunday Times*, 27 July 1980.

Television

The BBC Television Shakespeare. BBC, 1978-85.

The Taming of the Shrew, 1980.

Doctor Who. BBC, 1963-.

The Leisure Hive, 1980.

DVD Commentary, Lalla Ward, Lovett Bickford and Christopher H. Bidmead.

Warriors' Gate, 1981.

'The Dreaming'. DVD extra.

Production Information Subtitles, Martin Wiggins. DVD extra.

The Hitchhiker's Guide to the Galaxy. BBC, 1980.

Production Information Subtitles, Kevin Jon Davies. DVD extra.

Play for Today. BBC, 1970-84.

The Adventures of Frank, 1980.

Keep Smiling, 1980.

Playhouse. BBC, 1974-83.

The Journal of Bridget Hitler, 1981.

Top of the Pops. BBC, 1964-2006.

Film

Aldrich, Robert, dir, *Kiss Me Deadly*. Parklane Pictures, United Artists, 1955.

Carpenter, John, dir, *Dark Star*. Jack H Harris Enterprises, Bryanston, 1974.

Cocteau, Jean, dir, *La Belle et la Bête*. DisCina, 1946.

Cocteau, Jean, dir, *Orphée*. Andre Paulve Film, Films du Palais Royal, DisCina, 1950.

Cocteau, Jean, dir, *Le Testament d'Orphée*. Cinédis, Les Editions Cinégraphiques, 1960.

Conn, Peter, dir, 'Blame it on the Boogie'. Music video, Epic, 1978.

Godley, Kevin, and Lol Crème, dir, 'Fade to Grey'. Music video, Polydor, 1980.

Grant, Brian, dir, 'To Cut A Long Story Short.' Music video, Chrysalis, 1981.

Joyce, Paul, dir, *The Goad*. Twin-Digit Productions, 1965.

Joyce, Paul, dir, *The Engagement*. Memorial Enterprises, 1970.

Joyce, Paul, dir, *The Day the Call Came*, Blackjack Productions, 1973. Incomplete footage in BFI archive.

Kozintsev, Grigori, dir, *Hamlet*. Lenfilm Studio, Pervoe Tvorcheskoe Obedinenie, 1964.

Kubrick, Stanley, dir, *2001: A Space Odyssey*, Metro-Goldwyn-Mayer, 1968.

Mallet, David, and David Bowie, dir, 'Ashes to Ashes.' Music video, RCA, 1980.

Resnais, Alain, dir, *L'Année Dernière à Marienbad*. Cocinor, Terra-Film, Cormoran Films, Precitel, Como-Film, Argos-Films, Les Films Tamara, Cinétel, Silver Films, Cineriz, 1961.

Scott, Ridley, dir, *Alien*. Twentieth Century Fox, 1979.

Schaffner, Franklin J, dir, *Planet of the Apes*. Twentieth Century Fox, 1968.

Visconti, Luchino, dir, *Death in Venice*. Alfa Cinematografica S.r.l., Warner Bros., 1971.

Welles, Orson, dir, *Touch of Evil*. Universal, 1958.

Welles, Orson, dir, *The Trial*. Paris-Europa Productions, Hisa-Films, Finanziaria Cinematografica Italiana, 1962.

Welles, Orson, dir, *Othello*, Scalera Film, 1951.

Stage Plays

Beckett, Samuel, *Act Without Words II*, 1956.

Radio

The Babylon Run. Manchester Piccadilly Radio, 1980.

The Dissolution of Dominic Boot. BBC Light Programme, 20 February 1964.

Hi-Fi Theatre. BBC Radio 4, 1978-79.

 An Alternative to Suicide, 16 November 1979.

Hunters' Moon. Manchester Piccadilly Radio, 1979.

The Last Rose of Summer. Manchester Piccadilly Radio, 1978.

Saturday Night Theatre. BBC Radio 4, 1943-98.

 The Humane Solution, 17 March 1979.

Visual Art

Friedrich, Caspar David, *Dolmen in the Snow*. 1807.

Friedrich, Caspar David, *The Abbey in the Oak Wood*. 1809-10.

Friedrich, Caspar David, *The Monk by the Sea*. 1808-10.

Friedrich, Caspar David, *Monastery Graveyard in the Snow*. 1817-19.

Friedrich, Caspar David, *The Wanderer Above the Sea of Fog*. 1818.

Friedrich, Caspar David, *Woman Before the Rising Sun (Woman Before the Setting Sun)*. 1818.

Friedrich, Caspar David, *Two Men Contemplating the Moon*. 1819-20.

Web

Farndale, Nigel, 'Sir Tom Stoppard Interview'. *The Telegraph*, 19 January 2010.
https://www.telegraph.co.uk/culture/theatre/7019256/Sir-Tom-Stoppard-interview.html. Accessed 31 December 2018.

Gallagher, Stephen, 'Creating the Audio Drama'. *Hauling Like a Brooligan*, 15 October 2012.
http://brooligan.blogspot.com/2012/10/creating-audfio-drama.html. Accessed 3 May 2018.

Hadoke, Toby, 'Christopher Bidmead: Part 1'. **Toby Hadoke's Who's Round** #147. https://www.bigfinish.com/releases/v/toby-hadoke-s-who-s-round-147---christopher-h-bidmead-part-1-1421. Accessed 20 January 2018.

Hadoke, Toby, 'Christopher Bidmead: Part 2'. **Toby Hadoke's Who's Round** #148. https://www.bigfinish.com/releases/v/toby-hadoke-s-who-s-round-148---christopher-h-bidmead-part-2-1422. Accessed 20 January 2018.

Hadoke, Toby, 'Stephen Gallagher: Part 1'. **Toby Hadoke's Who's Round** #166. https://www.bigfinish.com/releases/v/toby-hadoke-s-who-s-round-166---stephen-gallagher-part-1-1490. Accessed 4 August 2017.

Hadoke, Toby, 'Graeme Harper: Part 1'. **Toby Hadoke's Who's Round** #213. https://www.bigfinish.com/releases/v/toby-hadoke-s-who-s-round-213---graeme-harper-part-1-1720. Accessed 29 March 2018.

Hadoke, Toby, 'Paul Joyce: Part 1'. **Toby Hadoke's Who's Round** #165. https://www.bigfinish.com/releases/v/toby-hadoke-s-who-s-round-165---paul-joyce-part-1-1488. Accessed 29 July 2017.

Hadoke, Toby, 'Paul Joyce: Part 2'. **Toby Hadoke's Who's Round** #167. https://www.bigfinish.com/releases/v/toby-hadoke-s-who-s-round-167---paul-joyce-part-2-1494. Accessed 29 July 2017.

Horgan, John, 'David Bohm, Quantum Mechanics and Enlightenment'. *Scientific American Blog Network*, 23 July 2018. https://blogs.scientificamerican.com/cross-check/david-bohm-quantum-mechanics-and-enlightenment/. Accessed 28 October 2018.

McEwan, Ian, 'Ian McEwan Writes about His Television Plays'. *London Review of Books*, vol. 3 no. 2, 5 February 1981. https://www.lrb.co.uk/v03/n02/ian-mcewan/ian-mcewan-writes-about-his-television-plays. Accessed 27 August 2018.

Mulkern, Patrick, *'The Leisure Hive'*. *Radio Times*, 13 March 2011. https://www.radiotimes.com/news/2011-03-13/the-leisure-hive/. Accessed 19 January 2019.

Newnham, Bernard, 'Inlay, Overlay and CSO'. *A Tech-Ops History in Stories and Pictures*. http://tech-ops.co.uk/next/inlay-overlay-and-cso/. Accessed 14 October 2018.

Panos, Leah, 'Mixing Genres in the Studio: Playhouse: The Journal of Bridget Hitler (BBC 2, 6/2/81)'. *Spaces of Television*, 20 February

2014. http://blogs.reading.ac.uk/spaces-of-television/2014/02/20/mixing-genres-in-the-studio-playhouse-the-journal-of-bridget-hitler-bbc2-6281/. Accessed 10 July 2018.

Press Association, 'Neil Gaiman: "My **Doctor Who** experience left me with a bad taste in my mouth"'. *The Telegraph*, 3 October 2018. https://www.telegraph.co.uk/on-demand/2018/10/03/neil-gaiman-doctor-experience-left-bad-taste-mouth/. Accessed 9 February 2019.

Rolinson, David, '(Times and) Spaces of Television - **Doctor Who**: Warriors' Gate (1981)'. *British Television Drama*, *23 November 2013*. http://www.britishtelevisiondrama.org.uk/?p=4228. Accessed 22 September 2018.

Smart, Billy, '**Doctor Who**: *Warriors' Gate* (1981), Jean Cocteau and the Realm of Videographic Fantasy'. *Spaces of Television*, 6 September 2013. http://blogs.reading.ac.uk/spaces-of-television/2013/09/06/warriors-gate-jean-cocteau-and-the-realm-of-videographic-fantasy/. Accessed 14 September 2018.

Storoy, David, 'David Bohm, Implicate Order and Holomovement'. *Science and Nonduality*, first published August 2014. https://www.scienceandnonduality.com/david-bohm-implicate-order-and-holomovement/ Accessed 18 August 2018.

Whittington, Karl, 'Caspar David Friedrich's Medieval Burials'. *Nineteenth-Century Art Worldwide* 11, no 1, Spring 2012. http://www.19thc-artworldwide.org/spring12/whittington-on-caspar-david-friedrichs-medieval-burials. Accessed 27 October 2018.

Young, Graham, 'David Rose talks of his time with BBC Birmingham at Pebble Mill'. *Birmingham Post*, 23 September 2009. https://www.birminghampost.co.uk/news/local-news/david-rose-talks-time-bbc-3940219. Accessed 27 August 2018.

ACKNOWLEDGEMENTS

I would like to thank the staff at the BBC Written Archives Centre (especially Louise North), and Simon Wilson and the staff at the University of Hull Archives at the Hull History Centre for their help with the production documentation at the BBC and accessing Stephen Gallagher's archive.

I am also particularly grateful to director Paul Joyce and writer Stephen Gallagher for their enthusiastic support and finding time to discuss *Warriors' Gate* and the rest of their work, answer questions and provide additional material.

For pointing me in various directions, sharing research, offering insights and friendship I also thank Graham Allan, Jon Arnold, David Brunt, Kevin Jon Davies, Ian Greaves, Toby Hadoke, Gareth Kavanagh, Jonathan Morris, Andrew O'Day, Ian Potter, David Rolinson and John Williams. I am much indebted to Philip Purser-Hallard, Stuart Douglas and Paul Simpson for their patience, understanding and editorial acumen when faced with a late and lengthy manuscript.

BIOGRAPHY

Frank Collins graduated from the School of Art and Design at the University of South Wales and completed an MA in Fine Art at the University of Reading.

He is the author of *Doctor Who: The Pandorica Opens – Exploring the Worlds of the Eleventh Doctor* (Classic TV Press, 2010) and 'Monsters Under the Bed: Gothic and Fairy-Tale Storytelling in Steven Moffat's Doctor Who' in *Doctor Who – The Eleventh Hour* (IB Tauris, 2014).

His essays are published in Arrow Video's Blu-ray releases of *Withnail and I*, *The Count Yorga Collection*, and *Woody Allen: Seven Films (1986-1991)*, he has contributed reviews and features to the British Television Drama, MovieMail, Television Heaven, Tachyon TV and Behind the Sofa websites, and he currently writes film and television reviews for Frame Rated.

Coming Soon